To:
Delaine Eastin,

Compliments

Dr. Nita West

10/31/95

RAISING ACHIEVERS

NITA WEIS, PH.D.

RAISING ACHIEVERS

A Parent's Plan for Motivating Children to Excel

BROADMAN
& HOLMAN
PUBLISHERS

Nashville, Tennessee

4261-60
0-8054-6160-4

Dewey Decimal Classification: 371.4
Subject Heading: Educational Counseling \ Parenting
Library of Congress Card Catalog Number: 94-30984

Unless otherwise noted, Scripture quotations are from the King
James Version of the Bible. Passages marked NIV are from the
Holy Bible,
New International Version, copyright © 1973, 1978, 1984 by
International Bible Society; and NASB, New American
Standard Bible, © the Lockman Foundation, 1960, 1962, 1963,
1968, 1971, 1972, 1973, 1975, 1977; used by permission.

Library of Congress Cataloging-in-Publication Data
Weis, Nita, 1931–
    Raising achievers : a parent's plan for motivating children to
excel / by Nita Weis.
        p.   cm.
    ISBN 0-8054-6160-4
    1. Education—Parent participation—United States—
Handbooks, manuals, etc.   2. Christian education—United States
—Handbooks, manuals, etc. 3. Motivation in education—United
States—Handbooks, manuals, etc. 4. Self-esteem in children—
United States—Handbooks, manuals, etc. 5. Underachievers—
United States. I. Title.
    LB1048.5.W45   1995
    649'.68—dc20   94-30984
                                                          CIP

*T*o my Christian mother and father who probably never thought of themselves as exemplary parents, but were. To my children, Kevin, Kendall, Leesa, and Lori, who were the original recipients of my practice parenting and as adults are achieving in their own entrepreneurial areas. To my beloved husband, Allan, who has been a loving, supportive husband and step-parent to my four children, who encourages most of my ventures, and who also introduced me to the word processor!

Contents

Preface

*U*nderachievement is like a diamond in the rough, whereas achievement is a life-long process with many facets. My only purpose in writing *Raising Achievers* is to help you ensure that each facet of your child's "brilliance" shines through!

Acknowledgments

I would like to acknowledge and thank my family, friends, and colleagues who contributed encouragement, support, and many hours of reading, critique, and suggestions in preparing the final copy of *Raising Achievers*.

I especially wish to extend my gratitude to two colleagues and friends I've known for over a decade, Shirley Burns and Barbara Harty. They kept me "educationally" correct, coherent, and "readable" by proofreading my manuscript . . . and we're still friends!

Thanks and fond memories to Dr. Jules Untiedt and Dr. Dorothy Harris who encouraged me to believe in myself and to keep reaching.

Special thanks to all those at Broadman & Holman, especially Janis Whipple. Without her patience, guidance, and belief in the need for and the premise of *Raising Achievers*, the book may never have been published.

Introduction

*T*his book may upset your apple cart about your own child's achievement in particular and about education in general. You see, I believe there's a movement "at large" to develop a guilt-free world, and this mindset is seriously limiting the efficiency of public and private education in America.

Let me give you an example. Ask almost any parent about the causes of underachievement, and the response will be an accusatory finger pointing away from themselves. Each of us fills in the blanks from our own biases: government bureaucracy, social inequities, poverty, racial issues, family breakdown, etc. In other words, many parents do not assume personal responsibility for the education of their children.

Two out of three Americans interviewed think our schools are failing. More government money hasn't made a significant difference in the past ten years. Parents, it's up to us to take back control of our children's education. It is to this purpose that this book addresses itself.

It has been my experience that most kids really do want to learn and do well in school, and most underachieving kids can become productive students.

My goal for *Raising Achievers* (RA) is to help you turn your misbehaving, underachieving, poorly-motivated, reluctant-learning kids into successful school students.

The hardest part of my job is not *fixing* the child, but convincing parents that their child is *fixable*. I know what you're thinking: "But you don't know my child. Nothing short of a miracle is going to get my . . . rowdy Robert to settle down, reluctant Randy to finish his report, pouty Pamela to pay attention, silly Steven to stay on task, unhappy Hannah to do her homework, tired Teddy to turn off the TV, sullen Sharon to study Shakespeare, precocious Peter to complete his project, and distractible David to master division."

Well, as a matter of fact, I've met them all, and the good news is that they're all fixable! The bad news is that the longer reluctant learners are allowed to perform poorly, the less likely it is that you'll see them reach their potential.

A sports figure being interviewed on television was asked, "To what do you attribute your success?" His answer was not only wise, but alliterative: desire, dedication, determination, discipline, and decision-making. It's no coincidence that these are the same characteristics missing from the profile of most underachievers.

I don't claim to be a miracle worker or to have a bag of "achievement dust" to sprinkle on kids. But after working with over thirty-five thousand students during thirty years in education, I do have extensive knowledge and experience in diagnosing, assessing, and remediating a broad variety of achievement problems.

Parents, please don't be misled into thinking that you can entrust your child's school success solely into the teacher's hands, no matter how capable the teacher may be. I must confess that the best of us well-intentioned, qualified teachers simply do not have the time to teach the curriculum to approximately thirty students, act as private tutors, and have time left to adjust the attitudes and poor behavior that are associates of underachievement.

An achiever is one who purposefully reaches for and attains his goals! My goal is that within six to nine weeks you'll be on your way to becoming the proud parent of an achiever!

When you've signed the contract that follows, we'll ready to begin!

Parent Contract

I, _____, do solemnly resolve to
stop procrastinating. With RA's suggestions, I will begin
now, by identifying the problems my child has, and by
taking the necessary steps that will release his or her
potential for becoming an achiever!

_____

Parent Signature

_____

Date

P.S. Remember, dwelling on the mistakes of the past
puts change for the better on hold.

PART ONE

Problems and Causes
of
Underachievement

1

To Be or Not to Be an Achiever?

"We know what a person thinks
not when he tells us what he thinks,
but by his actions."

—ISAAC B. SINGER

*D*o any of the following cases sound familiar?

Scenario 1

(It's Monday evening, and Mom has just come in from her "outside" job and is putting in a load of laundry. Her teenage son, Paul, comes in from football practice.)

Mom: Have you started on your report for school yet?
Paul: It's not due until Friday.
Mom: That's only four more days. Didn't you tell me that assignment was a ten-page report?

Paul: I've got plenty of time. I'm working on it.

Mom: Let me see what you've done so far.

Paul: Well . . . it's not down on paper yet. But I've been thinking about it, and it won't take but a few minutes to write it out. Don't sweat it, Mom.

Scenario 2

(It's the evening of a typical school day. Mom is in the kitchen preparing dinner as her daughter, Darlene, comes running into the house with her friend.)

Mom: Finished your math homework yet?

Darlene: Ugh, *(hesitatingly)* no, I forgot to bring my math book home. But it's no big deal. I can do it in the morning before school.

Mom: But, your father saved time to help you tonight, and you know you're not a morning person.

Darlene: *(Shrugs shoulders.)* Trust me Mom. It's no big deal.

Scenario 3

(Fifteen-year-old Andrew has just come into the garage where his dad is doing some repair work on his car.)

Andrew: Dad, I need you to run me over to Jim's. We're gonna shoot some baskets and hang out.

Dad: Son, I'd love to oblige you, but your mother tells me that you probably will be getting a failing grade in Government if you don't improve. So, it looks like you need to be hitting the books instead of hanging out with your friends.

Andrew: *(angrily)* You and Mom don't want me to have any fun or any friends. I wish you'd just get off my back and stop treating me like a baby. Some of my friends' parents already let them drive, and some even have their own cars. I feel like a prisoner in my own home. *(Stalks out of the garage.)*

Scenario 4

(It's midyear. Debbie, a fourth-grader, has just handed her second progress report to her Mom. Hoping for a miracle, Mom's eyes scan the grades beside the core subjects. Regretfully, what she finds is a column of letters in which A, B, and C are conspicuously absent!

Mom: Debbie, what is this? You've been telling me that your grades were coming up. Nothing seems to be coming up except my blood pressure! Your father is going to be furious, and I am so disappointed. I don't know what to do with you or what to think.

Debbie: Mom, it's the teachers. They don't like me, and they never think anything I do is any good. They're not fair. I did have some good grades, and I did turn in some homework!"

(Mom shakes her head in disbelief, then sighs.)

Maybe you thought that I had a hidden camera in your home. No, these are typical examples, I assure you. From my experience, I can safely predict that there are many thousands of parents trying to cope with similar or worse problems. These scenarios are real cases of some behaviors that are *deadly* to achievement. Only the names have been changed, to protect those caught in the act of underachieving!

The Family Factor

The superintendent of one inner-city school district attributed the success of his students to the *family factor.* Fifty-eight percent of the kids in his school district did not speak English at home, yet they scored above the average. The secret is not money and fancy programs; it's getting parents involved in their children's education. It's getting them to listen to their kids read, monitor homework, attend open house, etc.

So, when so-called experts propose solutions to school problems without using the words *family, parents,* and *values,* look closely. It's parents who hold the keys to their kids' achievement. It's parents who set appropriate expectations, require the right attitudes, establish discipline and consequence parameters, and show loving interest and involvement in their children's education.

Raising Achievers is about what it takes to attain school success. Our task is to find those special ingredients that ensure academic achievement for all the children out there who are missing the mark. What's the secret? Is there a formula or a recipe for achievement?

I just happen to have a treasured copy of a yellowed, food-stained and crinkle-edged copy of a prize-winning recipe for you. Get out your pencils.
You'll be handing this one down to your grandchildren!

Prize-Winning Recipe for Achievement

First Mixture:
To any-size child, do the following:

> Add one rounded handful of self esteem.
> Measure in at least average ability.
> Sift in the right attitude,
> Alternating with appropriate decisions.
> Sprinkle with daily study sessions, and
> Add a generous helping of perseverance.

Second Mixture:
Next, interested parents are to add the following to the first mixture:

> Realistic discipline, and
> Carefully measured consistency.
> Garnish with a variety of select consequences.

Allow this mixture to rise in a warm environment. Then bake for a few years in a warm family oven of love and patience. You'll know that you've followed the recipe correctly when the mixture is golden brown and bubbly with achievement.

Parents, guess what *your* task is? You're right, it's pulling together just the right mix of these ingredients that will turn your little Billy or Susie into an achiever! Let's examine each of these briefly here, because they will be discussed in much more detail in chapters throughout the book. In order to turn underachievement around, parents and kids must become energetically involved in developing and embellishing the characteristics that lead to achievement. Notice I said "energetically" involved. Most of us possess pounds of knowledge, but put only ounces into practice.

---

75 percent of underachievement points directly at poor attitude and lack of perseverance!

Excluding the family factor, attitude and perseverance are two variables that most seriously affect achievement. I'll go even a step further and offer that 75 percent of underachievement points directly at poor attitude and lack of perseverance! In fact, most kids are ready to give up if they can't solve a problem or complete an assignment in thirty minutes!

While an attitude to learn is the responsibility of the child, the parent must motivate the child to exhibit the *right* attitude, not just *an* attitude. There is a difference. The child's responsibility is to learn, but the parent is the one who establishes and maintains a daily home-study regimen that is age- and ability-appropriate.

The child must learn perseverance, but it is the parent who sets the parameters that expect and require the child to learn according to his ability, and by his own effort, trial, and error. As the child uses his ability and learns through his own resilience, he is developing characteristics that nourish the growth of his self-esteem.

At some point, appropriate achievement parameters set by parents will call for discipline and consequences. Gene Bedley, a California principal of the year, says, "All behavior is maintained by its consequences." For discipline to work, there must be consequences that elicit the desired behavior.

We may warp a child's development
every time we make a decision
for him that he could have
made for himself.

Ineffective discipline is a critical factor in underachievement and is usually at the root of the child's inconsistency and lack of responsibility regarding homework. (See chapters 5 and 7 for whole-chapter treatment on discipline and homework.)

We are all products of our decisions, both good and bad. The only thing standing between most children and greatness is effort, and an essential part of effort is making the right decisions. We may warp a child's development every time we make a decision for him that he could have made for himself.

So if we want our children to be achievers, we need to provide opportunities for them to exercise decision making. Most important of all, let's make sure that they decide to do their best.

Characteristics of Underachievers

Ask any teacher for the characteristics of underachievers, and she'll rattle them off without missing a beat. Take a look at the following list of underachiever characteristics contrasted with achiever characteristics most frequently cited by teachers.

<u>Underachiever</u>	<u>Achiever</u>
Dependent	Independent
Procrastinating	Persevering
Lethargic	Energetic
Disinterested	Inquisitive
Irresponsible	Responsible
Stubborn	Obedient

At your last parent-teacher conference, did the teacher use any of the underachiever words in describing some problems your child was having was having? If not, this was probably no accident. Teachers are encouraged by their principals to use only positive terminology in describing students' behavior. For a more accurate translation of how the teacher really wanted to describe her behavior, refer to the descriptions following the "politically correct" terms.

Response Delay. Inactive, inert, needs to be jump started; synapses need regapping; never volunteers answers; a non-participant in classroom discussions or activities.

Problems with Task Completion. Unproductive, keeps circling the camp; appears to have lost his compass; or can't work without direct assistance or frequent monitoring.

Disinterested. Unemotional, unstirrable, self-satisfied, complacent.

Lethargic. Lazy, drowsy, unanimated, energy deficit, TV hangover, depressed.

Indecisive. Neutral, lukewarm, ho-hum effort, enthusiasm void.

Nonconformist. Noncompliant (stubborn), under-disciplined, spoiled, has "delusions of grandeur."

Underachievers Anonymous

In addition to these characteristics, I've observed many other problems during my tenure as an educator that also contribute to underachievement. I've narrowed down the list to twelve and named them Underachievers Anonymous—a 12-Step Program to Under-achievement!

1. Absenteeism

Parents of my clients are asked to bring the child's report card so I can see the school attendance profile alongside their grades. Erratic school attendance is frequently a serious factor in under-achievement. Out of approximately forty-five days in a grading quarter, it's not unusual to find that an underachiever has been absent 25-30 percent of the time. Imagine missing twelve to fifteen days of teacher instructions, twelve to fifteen days of homework assignments for practice, and perhaps three to five tests and quizzes. Is it any wonder that the child's quarterly grades are reflections of his poor attendance?

Now, you may choose trips to Hawaii, Europe, the Near East, Far East, North Pole, South Pole, and parts in between; go camping, backpacking, skiing, or on a miscellany of other quasi-educational or family-renewal jaunts via hiking, bicycling, driving, flying, or hot-air ballooning. You can travel by water raft, sailboat, motor boat, yacht, cruiseline steamer, camel, horse, or donkey. Some of my young clients have logged more frequent-flier miles than our congressmen. This is all fine and good, but all should be planned for regular school holidays and summer vacations! Excuses that the trip has educational advantages that far outweigh what the classroom offers are dubious. Even for the average student, and especially for an underachiever, "elective" absenteeism should not be an option.

2. Over-Commitment and Scattered Focus

There are all sorts of activities and events—innocuous by themselves—that collectively usurp a child's available study time. I call them "time warps, study-space invaders, and interruptus miscellaneous"! No matter how wholesome, educationally beneficial, or family-enhancing, the accumulation of these circumstances, events, and interruptions insidiously robs kids of available and valuable planning and study time.

Let me give you an example. Andrea came to me for assistance in her junior year at a prestigious, private high school. She was making Cs and Ds even though she had above-average intelligence plus a private tutor since the third grade.

The results of my assessment revealed Andrea had an auditory-attention, short-term memory deficit. This meant that she had difficulty processing and remembering information she heard. Since Andrea was taking all advance-placement classes, and most of her teachers used the lecture method, her auditory-attention deficit was particularly significant.

In the first few sessions I discovered another factor in Andrea's underachievement—major over-commitment! One afternoon a week, she was a volunteer at a local hospital. She was also a star player on the girl's varsity volleyball team, a commitment requiring practice and night games. Because both her parents worked, and her younger sister didn't drive yet, Andrea had to drive her to all of her activities each week. Her already-full schedule also included church attendance and choir practice several times a week!

Briefly stated, Andrea's auditory-attention deficit, too many activities, too little time to do homework, and long-term dependence on her tutor were the primary factors in her underachievement.

When Andrea's parents came in to discuss the results of her tests, I expected them to feel relieved that her problem was not serious. Instead, I sensed disappointment that my diagnosis was not a multi-syllable, medical-sounding diagnosis.

Sometimes, parents give the impression that they would prefer that I found a learning-disability instead of suggesting that they need to make some changes in their family habits and activities. They would rather I solve the problem.

Parents, remember this regarding underachievement. It is definitely applicable in Andrea's case. *Underachievement is more often related to the parent-child relationship than it is to the teacher-student relationship.*

I offered a simple "achievement prescription" for Andrea: curtail some of her activities; tape the classroom lectures in her most difficult classes for later review; attend six sessions on study-skill techniques; and eventually, "terminate" her tutor.

Her parents opted for the six sessions, but rejected two of my suggestions. They refused to eliminate Andrea's tutor or any of her extracurricular activities. They felt the activities were direct lines to her self-esteem. Since her achievement was already considerably below her ability, they felt that taking away her tutor would further jeopardize her GPA and subsequently her chances for acceptance at her university of choice.

What her parents failed to recognize was the underlying issue: Andrea needed to learn how to learn on her own!

Sometimes parents' well-intentioned decisions actually short-circuit the child's academic achievement. One example of this is allowing the child's time to be so subdivided that he or she lacks the time it takes to become a good student.

Scattered focus, or what I call activity-hopping is a variation of over-commitment. Little Billy and Susie select one activity after another, demonstrating no stick-to-it-ive-ness following their choices. You know what I'm talking about. Kids want to join scouts or sign up for some sport, but their interest lasts just long enough for parents to buy the uniforms! Next thing you know, their musical genes start making harmony, and they beg to join the band or start music lessons, often because their best friends did. After a few weeks, this interest also wanes, or their best friend drops out. But the instrument payments continue! Sound familiar? With four kids of my own, I've been around this block a few times.

So how do we put a halt to "Today Billy's a budding Chopin; next week, he's a baseball man"? Have your child make a list of activities that interest him. For each activity, list some advantages and disadvantages, along with the weekly estimate of time each activity will take. Once you approve the cost of the activity, then assign a stick-with-it time frame for each one.

This approach not only allows Billy and Susie to learn the necessary steps for making good decisions, but it also may save you money! If we allow kids to go from one activity to another without giving the activity reasonable time and effort, this pattern of scattered focus may translate into a habit of not completing their school work either. Kids need lots of opportunities to learn from their mistakes, and how to make better decisions the next time around.

It may be helpful to remind your child that all professional skaters, pianists, musicians, and sports figures had to stick with their particular interest in order to perfect it. But don't hold your breath, because most kids' plans have a universal timeline—*today!*

3. Underdisciplined

Dr. Toni Grant, author and radio psychologist, once said that a child may become a Rhodes Scholar, brain surgeon, or Eagle Scout without an occasional spanking, but that parents shouldn't count on it.

Even Dr. "no-spanking" Spock claimed that kids learn quickly when parents mean business and when they are not going to be pushed around. He encourages parents to be firm, in spite of the fact that kids won't welcome it. Spock also has found that parents who expect their children to cooperate usually have cooperative kids!

Psychologist John Rosemond reports that an unstable family produces an uncooperative child who is always clamoring for attention. He found that adult-centered families are more likely to produce achievers. Kids look up to adults who pay attention to each other first.

Of all the parent seminars I conduct each year, the topic most often requested is, "Discipline Doo-Dah, Guidelines for School Success." In fact, *Raising Achievers* evolved as a result of my research and preparation for these presentations. My "Doo-Dah" seminars always include my list of Behavior Deadlies. These behaviors are frequent companions of underachievement and should be red-flagged for elimination.

Behavior Deadlies

Procrastination, Indecision: any delay tactic that has an element of "Later, alligator."

Laziness, Homework "Con Artist": a lack of self-motivation or initiative to do assigned chores or homework; often accompanied by dubious complaints of headaches and stomachaches; often says, "I can't" and "I don't know how."

Inconsistency: erratic attitude or effort toward hobbies, household chores, or school assignments; runs "hot 'n cold."

Disorganization: lackadaisical planning; lack of adherence to guidelines and timelines; misplacement of materials related specifically to schoolwork or chores; wears the facade of helplessness or "I forgot."

Noncompliance, Obstinacy, Stubbornness: commonly known as "digging the heels in"; outright refusal; willful (or won't-ful) at inappropriate times.

Arguing: mostly from not wanting to do something or not wanting to suffer the consequences for "missing the mark"; often marauding under the guise of explaining, excuse making, or stalling for time.

Denial: at its worst, closely associated with lying; at its best, a lack of awareness or failure to recognize that a problem exists.

4. Whiners, Complainers, Blamers, Forgetters, and Procrastinators

A common thread of underachievement among a majority of my clients is simply that they are lazy; they procrastinate, or lack the perseverance to get the task done. They whine, complain, or forget the materials necessary to complete the assignments. They're never too tired to stay up late watching TV, but always too tired to finish homework. They know from experience that their moms stand ready to help them when they get in a pinch. Cries of *emergency* and *ple-e-e-ase* bring the over-and-ever-protective "helicopter moms" swooping down, circling, hovering, rescuing Billy and Susie from their feigned homework emergencies.

Eventually, helicopter moms exhaust their "nesting patience" with their little homework fledglings. Complaints of stress, exhaustion, and no time for their husbands or themselves are expressed. After working all day, they come home to their night job—school with the kids! They join in the struggle with spelling words, mastering math facts, searching for answers to history and geography questions, writing book reports, constructing last-minute science projects, etc.

Parents, it's time, as Dr. Kevin Leman says, "to pull the rug out" from under our Billys and Susies and let them fall. I call it "cutting the homework tether," and the cutting ceremony should take place no later than the end of the third grade!

Unintentionally, parents who give too much help with homework actually sabotage achievement. They think they're helping, when in reality they're sending the wrong message back to the child's teacher. Teachers think that Billy and Susie have mastered fractions, when it's actually Mom and Dad who know fractions! When the teacher sees parents' mastery of a concept returned as the child's homework, this actually can prevent your child from receiving the additional instruction she may need.

5. Noncompliance and Stubbornness

A mother called me about her twelve-year-old son who lied about not having homework assignments when he did. On the rare occasions when he did any homework, it represented below-level effort for his gifted ability. She had finally resorted to sitting at his side during homework time to ensure that he was demonstrating quality effort.

The particular incident that precipitated her call to me was after the two of them had worked past midnight finishing a report, only to learn later from the teacher that he never turned it in. He finally admitted to throwing it in the trash before entering class! This sort of behavior is the epitome of noncompliance—a step beyond stubbornness.

A noncompliant child is the one who refuses by words or inaction to do what he is asked to do by those with recognized

15

authority. This refusal is not cute beyond age two, and should not be tolerated for a minute. The non-compliant child turns in a one-paragraph paper when the assignment specified a two-page effort. And contrary to liberal opinion, compliance does *not* quell creativity, individuality, and independent thinking! Point of fact is that a compliant child is learning what it takes to create quality work and develop independence.

6. Retention vs. Remediation

Most kids are made of the right stuff. Parents just need to give them a sufficient nudge (in some instances, maybe a shove) in the direction of responsibility. If you are the parent of an under-achiever, at some point in his underachievement, you'll have to decide what you're going to do about it. You really have only three choices: retention, remediation, or responsibility.

Let's talk about *grade retention* first. For the last ten years educational authorities have been pretty much in agreement that retention simply because the child is behind probably will do more harm than good. Furthermore, research shows that without unique intervention, retention offers very little benefit. An example of unique intervention could be a new (or better) teacher, a new school, a new curriculum, or a tutor. With very few exceptions, I'm not a devotee of retention.

In most cases of retention, the same class, same curricula materials, and the same teacher promise three things: another year of tuition if the child attends private school; a cocky attitude (he's a year older, been there, and done that); and boredom, which quickly escalates into a discipline problem!

One researcher reported that the trauma of retention on a child was second in severity to the death of a family member. Parents, please trust me and the majority of educational authori-ties, based upon our research and experience with retained kids. For years to come, your child will defend his older-age grade placement by announcing that he "failed" a grade.

Try *remediation* instead of retention, if at all possible. Take a simple, two-pronged achievement approach to the problem: (1) match the achievement expectations for your child with her ability; and (2) get her a qualified tutor in the areas of need until she gains the needed skills.

Select a teacher with a college major or minor in the subject being tutored, for the most time-and cost-efficient remediation. Experienced teachers provide excellent diagnostic-remedial tutoring in their fields of expertise, and they already have access to all the books and instructional materials needed.

An acceptable, and less-expensive, alternative to a teacher-tutor is a junior or senior high school student with a 4.0 GPA in the subject to be tutored. The student-tutor should work under the guidance of your child's teacher, who knows exactly what your child needs to learn. And teachers are more than glad to provide worksheets for practice in problem areas.

Just one word of caution if you plan to use a high school student. Make sure that the tutor is not only a good student, but also mature enough to keep friendship and "tutorship" separate. Ask for teacher recommendations if you decide to go with student tutors.

When you are paying a teacher or a student tutor, you need not feel shy about setting some guidelines. It is absolutely reasonable to expect a paid tutor to provide you with short-term objectives, weekly progress reports, a projected time line for "tutor-termination," and any home-study materials needed. In most cases, an effective tutor should be able to accomplish remediation within six weeks to a few months, unless the child has a serious achievement deficit.

7. Undermotivation and Under-Overprojection

The conservative estimation of children with learning disabilities is about 5 percent of the population. Yet the most frequently asked question by parents of underachievers is, "Does my child have a learning disability?" Remember Andrea's parents? Parents tend to think something serious has to be wrong when their child fails to get good grades. If a child misbehaves, she must be hyperactive. If he's slow learning how to read, he must be dyslexic. If she can't stay on task, she has an attention deficit disorder. We'll have more to say about "labels" in chapter six. Labeling a child with a learning disorder without some professional corroboration delivers a blow to the child's self-esteem and also provides him with an undermotivation crutch. My experience is that parents tend to *underproject* more than *overproject* the ability of the child. The underprojected child becomes the undermotivated child. Dr. David Viscott says undermotivated kids do whatever is tolerated by parents!

"Proceed with Caution" is a good plan when it comes to establishing expectations for your child. Schools do standardized testing each year to determine how kids are performing in terms of academic achievement. This kind of testing provides clues to how well your child is doing in comparison to her peers. If your child continues to fail in spite of reasonable and consistent effort, a more comprehensive learning ability assessment by a credentialed academic therapist or an educational or clinical psychologist is advised.

---

*"Undermotivated kids do whatever
is tolerated by parents!"
—Dr. David Viscott*

Intelligent kids can "fall through the cracks," even in a loving, caring home or school environment. It happened to me. I was born with a serious vision problem, which my parents were unaware of until my first-grade teacher brought it to their attention. So, I urge parents to make sure that the most basic aspects of the learning process are functioning prior to setting achievement expectations.

If, after a professional evaluation, you learn that your child is capable of making only Cs or less, then it is absolutely appropriate for you to expect him to perform only according to his ability. Under these circumstances, your best counsel may be helping him to focus his energy toward mastery of the survival skills needed for him to achieve a happy, respectable, and realistic degree of success. Expectations beyond what the child is capable of delivering produce stress and compromise his self-esteem.

8. Lazy, Homework "Con Artist"

Parents, dare to cut the homework "umbilical" and take back your life! Make your child responsible for her own homework. You've already finished school, so do you really want to go through it again, and again, and again, with each child? The more parents help with homework, the longer they will have to. This practice not only perpetuates the lack of responsibility development in the child, but also sends the wrong message to the teacher regarding mastery of material covered in homework assignments.

You'll know Billy and Susie are playing the homework con game if they use one or more of these responses to the question, "Have you done your homework?"

"I don't have any homework." "I did it at school." "I can't." "It's too hard." "I don't know how." "I did try." "I can't find the answer." "The teacher didn't show us how; he just said, 'Do it.'"

Parents, don't believe a word of it. Children do lie!

9. TV Addict

Youngsters in the U.S. spend about one third of their waking hours in front of the TV, according to 1993 research. This amounts to about forty hours a week watching programming or playing video games on the TV. Effects of the violence, sex, and drug messages aside, one can only imagine how much achievement would improve without it! Parents, isn't it time we did something about it?

I remember suggesting to the mother of a client of mine that she limit his TV watching. She said that she was unable to get the child to turn it off. I asked why she didn't turn it off, and her reply was the incredulous, "I do, but he just turns it on again!" Mind you, the kid glued to the tube was only in the second grade! If she can't control TV for her seven-year-old, what's she going to do when he's a teenager?

If you've lost control of the remote control, consider a "TV allowance." How about, no TV with less than a B average? Or offer the possibility of earning an extra thirty minutes or so for an A or one letter-grade improvement in a core subject—not P.E. class.

One psychologist suggests that children younger than about eight years of age should not be allowed to watch TV at all! I know of no research that shows that cartoon or sitcom "deprivation" leads to underachievement!

My personal bias is that the same guidelines for TV could be applied to video games. Video games haven't been around long enough for long-term studies, but researchers are already finding indications that long hours of video game playing produce behavioral changes such as increased irritability, aggressiveness, and anxiety, particularly when the games have violent content.

10. Poor Nutrition

Most parents are not chemists or nutritionists, but most of us know more about proper diet than we practice. That's why weight-loss plans, diet foods, health spas, and fitness tapes have continued appeal. But the focus here is on nutrition as it relates to learning.

Protein, better known to educators as "brain food," is for power learners. Carbohydrates provide quick sources of energy, but they also can produce drowsiness when the blood-sugar level falls. It's a fact that your child's eating habits can affect her learning.

A medical doctor lecturing on nutrition as it relates to learning said parents should make sure that their children's breakfast includes protein. The reason is that within one hour, that protein is supplying energy to the brain. He even suggested that parents might want to consider reversing the usual order of menus. Have the tuna sandwich for breakfast and the cereal and pancakes for dinner!

I picked up the following information about ice cream from a well-known yogurt shop. I make no claims for the accuracy of its content. I just thought parents might find it interesting. The article described how old-fashioned ice cream made with whole eggs, milk, and sugar probably did little harm. Then the comparison was made to present-day ice cream, whose ingredients may consist of synthetic and mass-produced products. Even if you take pride in being a label reader, the article pointed out that ice-cream manufacturers are not required by law to list the additives of ice cream! The following ingredients were listed: diethyl glycol, piperonal, aldehyde C17, ethyl acetate, butyraldehyde, amyl acetate, and benzyl acetate. These additives were used in mass-produced ice cream as substitutes for eggs, vanilla, cherry, pineapple, nut, banana, and strawberry flavorings.

The article concludes with the warning: "The next time you are tempted by a luscious-looking sundae or banana split, or ice-cream soda, think of it as a mixture of anti-freeze, oil, paint, paint remover, nitrate solvent, leather cleaner, and lice killer . . . you might not find it so appetizing." My rule is this: The more ingredients that I can't pronounce, the less likely I am to buy it!

11. Too Little Rest

A tired child is definitely less likely to become an achiever than is an alert child. Among the usurpers of energy and contributors to general fatigue are too many family activities, extracurricular commitments, TV, and video games. I've read reports of kids playing video games four to five hours straight, preferring the games to playing outdoors with friends.

Another fatigue factor is that because of parents' work schedules many kids are being picked up at five or six o'clock in the evening from extended day care, community centers, boys' or girls' clubs, and baby sitters. After-school child-care providers should provide staff and guidelines that include the monitoring of homework. There simply are not enough remaining hours to do quality homework after these kids get home, eat, and bathe. This is a *major factor* when both parents work and should be addressed by *all after-school care agencies!* Ask *loudly* for it; it's a reasonable request! This one factor alone would have an enormous, positive impact on the achievement of these kids and considerably reduce the homework pressures on parents.

12. Failure to Support Teachers

Parents, make it your responsibility to know what your child is supposed to be learning and what his progress is toward mastering this information. Set short-term objectives that ensure he is gaining proficiency on a daily basis.

Never criticize your child's teacher in front of your child. Withhold judgment and comments when "teacher tales" are brought home until you have some real evidence, such as two or three supporting witnesses!

Teachers usually make homework guidelines available in writing on a regular basis. If your child doesn't bring these home, ask the teacher for them. Failure to follow specific guidelines and timelines definitely will affect her grades. While teachers do not expect parents to do or correct the child's homework, they would appreciate a quick review of the homework, making sure that she at least followed the directions. Unfortunately, the teacher's directions may have become paper airplanes on the way home, or they may surface in early June at end-of-the-year locker clean out!

Post View and What Parents Can Do

- *Right attitude* and *perseverance* are responsible for approximately 75 percent of achievement!

- All behavior is maintained by its consequences.

- Procrastination and arguing are delay tactics.

- Avoid the urge to make decisions for your child that he can make for himself. This perpetuates underachievement and postpones the development of responsibility.

- Cut your child's "homework tether" by the end of third grade!

- Retention without unique intervention probably does more harm than good.

- Qualified, tutorial remediation is probably the shortest road to academic acceleration for your child.

- The undermotivated do whatever is tolerated by parents!

- Recognize that children will lie about homework assignments.

- Referring to the 12-Step Program to Underachievement in this chapter, list each of your child's underachievement problems here:

1. _____

2. _____

3. _____

4. _____

5. _____

2

What's Your Parenting Quotient?

"Train up a child in the way he should go and, when he is old, he will not depart from it."

—King Solomon

*W*e have the Food & Drug Administration to ensure the safety of our food and medicine and the Environmental Protection Agency to monitor such things as the quality of our air and water. Even students who work at fast-food restaurants get job training. So, I'm thinking that there should be an agency to warn us about the *Hazards of Parenting* or, at least, to make available extended warranties on our kids.

And what about this idea? Because no two kids are exactly alike, and because doctors have all that education and know so much, why don't they enclose an owner's manual along with their bill for the baby's delivery? Some of these little bundles are like ticking time bombs. You'd think that diffusing directions should be enclosed! It's not until after delivery that most of us begin to learn some very alarming facts about parenting. For example,

(1) The cost of raising a child, cradle through college, may well exceed $200,000! (2) Doctors say that anxiety, depression, and insomnia are common complaints of young mothers. (3) Psychologists report that marriages might suffer some adverse effects the first year or two following the birth of a child. Perhaps a teacher said it best: "Kids are harder to raise than orchids!"

Discipline plays a major part,
if not a leading role,
in most underachievement
problems.

So, once you're a parent, you'll need the wisdom of Solomon, the diplomacy of Jefferson, and the patience of Job. Your emotions will run the gamut of contradictions—from indescribable happiness to heart-wrenching sorrow, the thrill of accomplishment to inevitable failure, confidence and trust to anxiety and doubt, hope to despair. If you're a perpetually worried parent who can't decide whether to laugh or cry, collapse or explode, start a college fund for your kids or put a "For-Lease" sign on them, you're 100 percent normal. What the experts *really* are trying to say is that we can expect all our circuits to be busy and our search for serenity to be on hold for a decade or so, especially moms!

As if parenting were not enough of a challenge, many mothers find themselves joining the work force outside the home, in a society that still views mothers as the primary caregivers. Often one hears criticisms of these "working moms" for shirking their maternal roles as they seek to fulfill personal goals or to live more lavishly. However, what I've noticed through counseling working moms is that they pack a lot of guilt in their briefcases. This is especially true if they are unable to "keep all their ducks in a row."

It's been said, "Children are the enemy. Prepare for war!" But *Raising Achievers* shifts the focus to *underachievement* as the real enemy. Our agenda is to develop a "combat plan," with armor and ammunition for launching a full-scale attack on the problems that contribute to underachievement.

The "battle" analogy reminds me of the cable television series that I hosted several years after my own divorce. The six thirty-minute shows offered survival tips for divorced parents from a psychologist, a marriage-family-child counselor, two authors of books pertinent to our topic, a university professor, a famous divorce attorney, and a Marine Corp drill sergeant.

Each guest contributed many helpful ideas from personal expertise, but the segment that generated the most interest was on discipline. As a teacher I knew that discipline plays a major part, if not a leading role, in most underachievement problems. The drill sergeant confirmed that discipline is as important in the Marines as it is in the classroom! He said it was easy to spot the under-disciplined among his new recruits, and that it was much harder to shape them up. He emphasized the importance of stated rules of conduct, consequences, and discipline consistency for his enthusiastic audience of mostly single moms.

The reason women are so interested in discipline is found in statistics that tell us that 49 percent of households in the U.S. have a single female as head of the household. Other surveys report that a majority of the disciplining of children remains the responsibility of mothers, even in two-parent families.

If you would like to know what your present level of parent effectiveness is for producing an achiever, take the following simple pre-test. But, first, you have to promise me that you won't panic and send your kids off to Aunt Martha to raise if you're not pleased with your score. After you've read this book, you can take the test again. I'm sure your score will have soared!

Parenting Quotient Test

Directions: *Each* parent circles answers to each statement under the Yes, Sometimes, or No column. Add columns one and two together into one sum. Total column three and subtract this sum from the total of columns one and two to get each parent's Raw Score. Add the raw scores from each parent's test and divide by two to find your average Parenting Quotient. Single parents omit the last step.

Y	S	N	
8	4	1	I teach reverence for God and respect for self and others.
8	4	1	I compliment and hug my children and tell them that I love them frequently.
8	4	1	I model appropriate behavior before my children.
8	4	1	I acknowledge good behavior in each child and am consistent in administering appropriate consequences for the bad behavior.
8	4	1	My spouse and I set, post, and agree upon age-based behavior for each child.
8	4	1	My spouse and I have set, agreed, and discussed with each child, the achievement levels expected of them according to ability.
8	4	1	I require a daily, age-grade appropriate home-study regimen for each child.
8	4	1	I limit my child's extra-curricular activities.
8	4	1	I encourage and recognize personal and academic growth.
8	4	1	For responsibility development, each child has assigned chores.
8	4	1	I am patient and calm a majority of the time.
8	4	1	I love, lead, listen, and laugh with my child.
8	4	1	I allow my child to learn through perseverance, consequence, and failure.

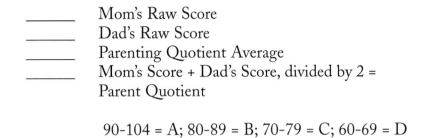

_____ Mom's Raw Score
_____ Dad's Raw Score
_____ Parenting Quotient Average
_____ Mom's Score + Dad's Score, divided by 2 =
Parent Quotient

90-104 = A; 80-89 = B; 70-79 = C; 60-69 = D

Expecting Responsibility

Most of the ideas and suggestions on discipline, as they relate specifically to achievement, will be found in chapters four and five. But for our getting-off-on-the-right-foot stage, at least the conceptual aspects of discipline and responsibility are appropriate here.

Self-discipline and responsibility are fundamental to achievement; and when early discipline and responsibility training begin at home, kids are being prepared for doing well in school. Teachers report that kids are much more adaptable to classroom structure and following directions when it's obvious that they've been exposed to these expectations at home. As parents, we must begin to provide for the child's responsibility development and disciplinary training early—the sooner, the better.

Children who become increasingly responsible for day-to-day chores in the home show an increase in their self-esteem, because they are learning new things. More difficult chores can be added gradually as the child matures, until he eventually knows how to do just about everything that it takes to run a home. That doesn't mean that we're going to expect the child to do all the chores all the time, but he should be learning how to do them. It is reasonable to expect twenty to thirty minutes a day of age-appropriate chores. And if this regimen is followed, our weekends are free of chores! Kids who complain the loudest about doing chores are often those who are responsible for the same chores all the time, so try varying chore assignments.

Making beds, picking up clothes and toys, keeping drawers neat, making school lunches, taking out trash, shopping for groceries, cooking, clearing the table, doing dishes, mopping floors, vacuuming, cleaning bathrooms, doing laundry, ironing, feeding the pets, cleaning the attic or garage, even cleaning the tile grout with a toothbrush, are all chores that make a house hum. These can and should be learned and mastered by all at an age-appropriate time.

Is Your Child a Statistic?

If you have an underachiever and think your situation is unique, I'd like you to review some startling statistics as proof of the scope of underachievement across America. These statistics should encourage you that you are a member of a "mega support group!" Crossroads in American Education, a twenty-year study funded by the Department of Education, followed the performance of about 1.4 million students. Math, science, and reading and writing performance of nine, thirteen, and seventeen-year-olds was studied. The following findings and recommendations were reported.

- Nine-year-olds: One-third could not read simple texts. One-quarter lacked beginning math skills or simple understanding of age-appropriate scientific principles.
- Thirteen-year-olds: More than one-third lacked adequate elementary math skills. Forty percent could not read passages at intermediate levels of difficulty, and only one-half displayed an understanding of basic scientific information.
- Seventeen-year-olds: Sixty-one percent had less than high-school level understanding of reading material. Almost one-half had no math skills beyond adding, subtracting, and multiplying of whole numbers.
- All age levels studied: Writing proficiency had not improved in ten years! The board's recommendation was that "more homework, higher-performance standards, and more course work in core subjects could help improve performance."

Other statistics note that America has over twenty-seven million adults who are unable to read and as many as sixty million more who could be classified as functionally illiterate. U.S. students continue to lag behind those in other nations on "virtually every qualitative measure." The State Education Performance Chart showed that an average of only 71 percent of students graduate nationwide from U.S. schools.

Reliable sources report that American students continue to perform poorly in math and science when compared with Japanese students. Spelling and writing skills of our high-school graduates continue to reflect their lack of linguistic ability. Transcripts show that far too many high-school and college students are opting for the "easy-ride" courses.

Money doesn't seem to be the answer either. For the year 1992, $425.5 billion was spent on education. According to a U.S. Department of Education press release, however, there has been no significant improvement in student achievement.

A Parent's Role

In a research sample of 2,512, reported in May 1992, two out of three Americans responded that public education is failing. We've lost confidence, and we want something done about it! These statistics are sobering and embarrassing. Assuming the research figures are correct, it follows that what has been done and is being done is not acceptable. It's going to be up to parents to see that the educational needs of our children are met.

You say, "But, I'm not a teacher. I pay my taxes to support schools. So why should I have to be so involved in my child's education?" My response is, "If you didn't have this right, you'd be fighting for it, because no one has the vested interest in your child's education that you do!"

There are basically only three requirements of parents for keeping their children from becoming a part of these educational statistics—ability, authority, and interest.

Raising Achievers includes the necessary guidance and information to increase parents' confidence in their ability to monitor kids' achievement.

Parents alone have the *authority* and responsibility to expect their child's school performance to match his ability level. Throughout the remaining chapters, parents will learn the fundamentals of discipline that are prerequisites for school achievement.

It is the exception rather than the rule for a child to become an achiever without having an *interested* parent. Get involved in your child's education, not just his homework. Attend school functions. Meet her teachers. Attend PTA meetings. Volunteer as often as your schedule allows. When parents are interested, kids are.

Psychologist William Glasser wrote in *Reality Therapy*, "Plausible as it may seem, we must never delude ourselves into wrongly concluding . . . that a delinquent child broke the law because he was miserable . . . not because he was angry or bored . . . but because he was irresponsible." Each of us as parents must accept parenting as a lifetime responsibility and privilege.

Post View and What Parents Can Do

- Recognize underachievement as your child's enemy.

- Use your *ability, authority,* and *interest* to launch a full-scale attack on the causes and problems of your child's underachievement.

- Affirm that self-discipline and responsibility are fundamental components of achievement.

- Acknowledge that early training of your child in the home prepares him to do well in school.

- Assign your child twenty to thirty minutes of age-appropriate daily chores, because there is a correlation between daily chores and increased self-esteem.

- Be aware that students in America lag behind those in other nations on virtually every qualitative measure, and government money has not proved to be the answer.

- Join the two out of three Americans who think education in America is failing, then decide to do something about it.

- Start by assessing and expecting *ability performance* from your own child.

- Establish disciplinary guidelines for your child which give priority status to an *attitude to learn.*

- Enter your Parenting Quotient here: _____.

Self-esteem and
the Passive Learner

*"It's hard to rise above
the pictures planted in our heads
as children."*

—ANONYMOUS

Self-esteem is a subject much discussed in modern society. Educators have long known that self-esteem is a critical factor in achievement. As a matter of fact, you may have been told that your child's lack of self-esteem is a reason for his underachievement. In this chapter we will discuss the origins and definition of self-esteem, as well as the role of parents in its positive development.

Bought, Caught, or Taught?

Can we buy self-esteem? Is there a guaranteed formula? I suspect if the secret to a self-esteem elixir existed, it would not only be a marketable product, but also more in demand than a McDonald's franchise! Sometimes we adults act as though we can buy self-respect and recognition as we strive to keep up with the Joneses. Should it come as a surprise when our children attempt to buy popularity and friends by plying them with gifts or by compromising better judgment in order to be one of the "in" crowd?

When parents are stretchers and reachers, their kids usually are not afraid of challenges.

Now, catching self-esteem might be a little more plausible, that is, if parents were "carriers." Parents certainly aren't perfect. But, if on a fairly regular basis, our kids see us practicing our beliefs and principles, excited about learning new things, challenging ourselves, and approaching problem-solving positively, then it's more than possible that they might "catch" some self-esteem characteristics. When parents are stretchers and reachers, their kids usually are not afraid of challenges. On the other hand, if kids see parents as couch slouches, rut huggers, and poor stress managers, they will opt for the comfort zone.

Can self-esteem be taught? Yes, if we teach them correctly. What is it that makes some wake up with vigor and enthusiasm, ready to take on the day, its challenges and opportunities? The answer is, "thinking right." A wise man said long ago, "As he thinketh in his heart, so is he." (Prov. 23:7). Many years later, the apostle Paul wrote, "Whatsoever things are true . . . honest . . . just . . . pure . . . lovely . . . of good report . . . think on these things" (Phil. 4:8).

Our thoughts influence, and to a great degree, control, our behavior. The best-selling author, Tony Robbins, recommends "no stinkin' thinkin'" in his book *Unlimited Power*. If your child is a negative thinker, my suggestion is that he post a "No Dumping Here" sign beside his bedroom mirror, as a daily reminder! Others are only too happy to oblige us with daily *dumping*, so why do it to ourselves?

One of the greatest self-esteem boosters we can give our children is happy, pleasant, positive parents who make sure kids' days at least begin positively. We either send our kids off to school with a smile in their hearts, or we accept some of the blame and guilt for their low self-esteem and underachievement.

For the next few pages, I'd like you to look at self-esteem through a new set of lenses and maybe get a new perspective. I've selected four questions to focus our discussion of self-esteem: What is the essence of self-esteem? What role do parents play in the development of the child's self-esteem? How can parents know when the child's self-esteem is "in distress"? What steps can parents take to enhance self-esteem growth?

What Is Self-Esteem?

So what is this elusive thing called self-esteem, and how does it relate to school achievement?

Self-Discovery

If we go to the dictionary for the meaning of self-esteem and its synonyms—self-image and self-concept—we find simple, concise definitions, like "belief in oneself and one's abilities, self-respect, and self-worth." I personally prefer the term self-discovery, because it implies an ongoing awareness and development of one's true potential, character, and motives. This term also presumes that each person is a project in progress by his Creator, with God continually reshaping His design.

Therefore, the whole concept of self-esteem is much more than the brief dictionary definition, and more than the current socio-educational buzzword. It's far more than merely a desirable characteristic. Self-esteem is the very essence of one's personality, maybe even the cornerstone of achievement.

We parents have very little control over some of the environmental influences that affect our children's self-esteem. But from my perspective both as an educator and a parent, I'd like for us to explore some components of self-esteem development over which parents do have some control and influence.

Belief in God

Eight out of ten people in America say the Bible is the Word of God. In 1991, a City University of New York study revealed that nearly 90 percent of the American people identify themselves religiously as Christians or Jews. This same study reported that only 7.5 percent claimed no religion.

Now, put on your glasses, here comes the *new perspective*. I know that I'm taking a chance of alienating the small part of the population who professes no religious preference, but I'm going to say it anyway. It's my contention that a healthy self-concept begins with a belief in God, and that one can't develop a truly healthy self-image and ignore the One in whose image he was made.

God wants our children to be
achievers, and He's promised
to be their learning partner:

It's true that philosophers, scientists, and the religious community do not all agree with me, or each other, for that matter. But for centuries, all have debated similar questions. Who are we? Where did we come from? Why are we here? Is there a basic code of behavior? Is this life all there is?

William J. Bennett, former U.S. Secretary of Education and author of *The De-Valuing of America,* shares a similar view. He espouses strong beliefs in the benefits of religion on education. He even supports voluntary school prayer and posting of the Ten Commandments in schools, concluding that when we have disdain for our religious tradition, we have disdain for ourselves.

Isn't it about time that the 90 percent of us who profess a belief in God stop being the silent majority when it comes to the education of our children? Don't you think that we're in a sad state of affairs when it's okay to pass out condoms in schools, but it's not okay to pray there?

I've not conducted scientific research into whether a relationship exists between a belief in God, high self-esteem, and school achievement, but my sense is that they are related. My bias comes from personal experience through my private counseling practice, which serves clients from both public and religious schools. My conclusion is that those who believe in God and are churchgoers tend to have a higher motivation to excel and a greater respect for learning.

There's still another advantage for parents of kids brought up in the church. Parents can defer to a higher power regarding the academic standards they've set for their kids. We can remind them that God wants them to be achievers, and He's promised to be their learning partner: "If any of you lack wisdom, let him ask of God" (Jas. 1:5). Don't worry. Your kids will not be eager to debate with God. (For additional references, see Prov.: 3:13; 4:7; 10:14; 12:1; and 18:15.)

All major religions make references to the benefits of knowledge and good stewardship of one's time and talents. Of course, parents will be guided by their own particular beliefs as they teach their children about the stewardship of one's mind for achievement.

I have no doubt that there are those who achieve without high self-esteem and without a belief in God. But I stand behind my statement that a belief in God gives kids a definite self-esteem edge. The Bible also provides parents with an exemplary guide for teaching values, training, correcting, and setting standards of excellence and achievement.

What Role Do Parents Play?

What role do parents play? A significant and essential one. Here's where the process hits a snag. I've found that there are at least three problems that can prevent parents from assuming a more active role in the development of their children's self-esteem.

First, parents lack a hands-on understanding of self-esteem that enables them to break self-esteem down into workable components.

A second problem is that there is no checklist that gives parents early warning that their child's self-esteem might be in jeopardy. There are formal inventories for professionals to use in determining if the child's self-esteem is "intact," but these standardized tests are not generally available to parents.

A third problem arises when a parent learns that his child's self-esteem is in distress, but he has no practical guidelines for providing early intervention. While parents readily agree that self-esteem is important, they often express confusion about how to improve it.

How Can Parents Detect Self-Esteem in Distress?

Most of us are familiar with the Scholastic Aptitude Test (SAT) that is given to high school students to predict college success. Most colleges and universities use SAT scores as one measure of the student's acceptance criteria.

But how about those kids who have a history of low self-esteem? By the time they reach their teens, it's probably a little late to predict college success. Because there is general agreement concerning the importance of self-esteem to success and school achievement, why not give self-esteem assessments during the critical years—three to five years of age? And why not monitor the development of self-esteem periodically throughout the child's physical development?

I try to practice what I preach, so each of the thousands of kids tested each year by my staff is given a Self-Esteem Inventory. We have children answer questions that indicate whether or not their environments are providing the essential elements that will lead to healthy self-esteem development.

During the developmental stages of our Self-Esteem Inventory, professionals agreed that the survey must provide information on the most basic fundamentals of self-esteem:

Q. Can the child spend some time alone and not feel sad? Is the child a nice person to be with? Does he enjoy his own company?

Q. Does the child have a significant parent role model, a hero to emulate?

Q. Does the child have a nurturing environment that supports open communication?

Q. Does the child have an environment that recognizes her accomplishments and makes her feel good about them?

Q. Does the child have an environment that loves the child, apart from his accomplishments?

Q. Does the child have an environment that allows for rule-bending on special occasions?

Q. Does the child have an environment that includes interaction with children and adults, one that provides opportunities for her to hone her relationship skills?

If you'd like to check your child's present self-esteem level, ask a special, non-family person to administer one of the following tests that is age-grade appropriate.

The examiner reads the questions to preschoolers through fourth graders, as this allows an opportunity to clarify any questions. Remind the child that there are no right or wrong answers. *The results are not to be shared with the child.*

Level 1. Self-Esteem Inventory

For Preschool through 4th Grade, ask these questions.

Y S N   Circle answers. Y = Yes, S = Sometimes, N = No

1 3 5   1. When you're left with a babysitter, do you feel sad?

1 3 5   2. Do you think other kids have nicer families than you do?

1 3 5   3. Do you do lots of things that make other people and your family mad at you?

5 3 1   4. Do other kids like to play with you?

5 3 1   5. If you see something in a store that you want, do you ask your parents to get it for you?

5 3 1   6. When it's time to go to bed, and a special show is on TV, would you ask to stay up a little longer?

5 3 1   7. When you grow up, would you like to be like your Mom (for girls)? Dad (for boys)?

NOTE: Examiners, be sure to clarify that the question has nothing to do with the type of job Mom or Dad has, but being a nice person like Mom or Dad.

1 3 5   8. Are other kids mean to you?

5 3 1   9. Are grownups nice to you?

_____   Raw Score: the sum of circled responses.

* High = 37-45; Average = 25-36; Low = 0-24

DO NOT ALLOW THE CHILD
TO SEE THIS SCORING!

Level 2. Self-Esteem Inventory

For 5th through 12th Grade, ask these questions.

Y	S	N	Circle answers. Y = Yes, S = Sometimes, N = No
1	3	5	1. When you're alone, do you feel sad?
1	3	5	2. Do you think that other people have better luck than you do?
1	3	5	3. Do you do lots of things that make your friends mad at you?
5	3	1	4. Do most people like you?
5	3	1	5. For Christmas or your birthday, do you drop hints to your family about gift ideas?
5	3	1	6. Do you spend money on yourself for things you don't really need?
5	3	1	7. Do you feel good about your accomplishments?
1	3	5	8. Do other people treat you unfairly?
5	3	1	9. Are most people nice to you?

PARENTS: If your child is a good reader, delete the scoring code, photocopy the test, and allow him to take the test by himself.

_____ Raw Score: the sum of circled responses.

* High = 37-45; Average = 25-36; Low = 0-24

DO NOT ALLOW THE CHILD TO SEE THIS SCORING!

43

How Can Parents Enhance the Child's Self-Esteem?

Did the survey indicate that your child's self-esteem "pilot light" is burning low? If so, the following seven suggestions will take the self-esteem basics and translate them into action steps for "re-igniting" his self-image.

Requiring the Right Image

Of course, parents will set their own standards of excellence for their children, according to their own religious beliefs and values. But, as was stated earlier, America's religious consensus is about 90 percent Christian and Jew. The majority would probably agree that "image" development begins with respect for God, parents, self, and others. Learning the value of honesty, wisdom, responsibility, a work ethic, and helping others adds a third dimension to self-image.

While we're on the subject of image, let's not forget to include the child's personal appearance and also his private space —his bedroom! It was reported that the wearing of school uniforms was shown to actually change some kids' behavior! Let's take this logic just a tad further. If kids' rooms looked a little more like "study stations" rather than video arcades, their grades would improve, probably at "warp" speed!

Communicating Your Expectations

Kids don't know what we expect of them unless we verbalize it. Let's make it clear that these learning and achievement expectations have top priority status. And by the end of first grade, these expectations should be in place! Yes, you read it right, *first grade!* When we set achievement standards for our kids that are below their ability, then later raise these standards, we send them mixed messages and insult their intelligence.

Use charts as visual reminders of your child's progress toward his goals. No self-respecting teacher would be without her charts. In fact, God Himself was probably one of the original chart makers! He commanded His people in the Old Testament to teach His statutes and ordinances to their children by (paraphrased)

44

"writing them on the posts of their houses as well as on the gates," (Deut. 6:1-9) so children would see them daily. As soon as your child can read, post her objectives and goals. For prereaders, devise creative ways to designate their chores and objectives. Pictures cut from magazines are great if you're like me—artistically challenged!

Starting the Gimme-Five Plan

If you want to see a child's self-esteem improve quickly, try my *Gimme-Five Plan.* Ask your child's teacher to give you a list of what he needs to learn. Select and assign him five new things to learn each day. This activity is not only age appropriate, but it also will pace his achievement. Some examples of short-term objectives could be five new spelling words, five new math facts, five geography, history, or science facts, or five new vocabulary words. Educators report a high correlation between learning and increased self-esteem. So allow your child to experience pride through his accomplishments.

Require proof that he's mastered his five facts before meal time each evening. No facts, no food! If he goes into "underachiever's shock," remind him that the Good Book says, (paraphrased) "If any would not work, he neither should eat" (2 Thess. 3:10). It's our responsibility as parents to impress upon our kids that their work assignment and job description is to learn. When we establish learning as the priority, so will they!

Correcting Without Damaging the Ego

Kids tend to live up to the expectations set for them by those significant to them—their parents, teachers, coaches, peers, and even older siblings! Someone once said, "It is hard to rise above the pictures planted in our minds as children." I cringe when I hear thoughtless remarks made to a child that can damage his self-image. Here are a few such remarks:

> "Why can't you be more like your sister?
> She always gets good grades."

> "I'm embarrassed to face your teachers."

"Your homework is always so sloppy."

"You never try."

"Why don't you care about anything?"

"Why do you always wait until the last minute?"

"Why are you always so disorganized?"

A more positive, objective, and result-oriented approach would be to suggest this: "You're not getting the grades because you are not organized. Starting now, you're to begin your assignments with enough lead time to show what we know you're really capable of doing."

When we are correcting children, we need to remind ourselves to separate the *offense* from the *offender*. And avoid sibling comparisons, which create hostility between children. These comparisons actually can have a negative effect on their motivation to achieve.

Giving "Realistic" Compliments

Mark Twain once said that he could go two whole months on one good compliment. By contrast, it's been estimated that it takes nine compliments to wipe out one negative remark. I remember reading somewhere that the national compliment average is one-half of a compliment a week! Just as thoughtless remarks can cause irreparable damage to kids' egos, sincere compliments can have a positive effect on self-esteem.

Research also has shown that low self-esteem is related to child abuse, spouse abuse, and drug abuse. A negative self-image has also been linked to violence, crime, teenage pregnancy, and academic failure. California assemblyman John Vasconcellos, a long-time advocate of self-esteem, had this to say: "How long before we stop dragging dead bodies from the river, instead of fixing the bridge?" It be wiser for us to focus on the problem rather than the person, because problems are easier to fix than damaged egos.

Often, all that is needed for kids to release their inborn achievement potential is a healthy self-concept. No matter how nonchalant they seem, kids do not feel good about doing poorly in school, where their achievement is under scrutiny twelve to eighteen years of their young lives! School is one of a child's most significant environments.

Sometimes parents heap inflated praise upon their children in a desperate attempt to quick-fix their self-esteem. For example, a client of mine took her child to Disneyland for getting an A on one spelling test! In the same way, you don't reward little Bobby for staying within the margins of his notebook paper. That takes away his incentive to pursue a more arduous task, like actually writing something of substance on his paper!

It's been estimated that it takes nine compliments to wipe out one negative remark.

Let's give kids realistic compliments for real progress toward their goals. Inflated or unearned praise is actually counterproductive to self-concept growth. Kids quickly see through this inflated praise facade, and they may even lose a little respect for us when we fail to expect of them what they are capable of doing.

Providing Good Role Models

Another aspect of self-esteem development is related to the child's peer group. As you know, peers exert enormous influence upon our children, and we've all heard horror stories about kids having "gone bad" as a result of bad peer influence. Dr. James Dobson found that the strong-willed child was more peer dependent than the compliant child by a ratio of 58 to 24 percent! In light of this research alone, an obedient child has an advantage at overcoming inevitable peer pressure.

One way that parents can help in providing kids with good role models is to arrange opportunities for them to come in contact with adults who have exciting and interesting careers. Enriching a child's role-model environment will contribute subtle and long-lasting influences, well worth your effort.

Eliminating Underachievement Crutches and Problems

Experienced teachers know what your child is capable of doing and can provide you with this information at no cost. If your child has a more serious problem, however, it would be wise to get a professional evaluation by an educational or clinical psychologist. Ask your child's principal for a referral or look in the Yellow Pages of your telephone book for these resources.

Parents, once you are satisfied that you know the ability of your child, expect him to work at (or very near) his achievement level. This level is reasonable and is not negotiable. If the child is allowed to select his own effort and achievement levels, he has usurped the position that only the parent and teacher should occupy.

From my research, and as an academic therapist for many years, I've collected quite an array of problems that kids (and parents) frequently lean on as crutches or excuses for underachievement. Here are three of the most commonly used crutches.

Birth Order. Many parents I've counseled excuse their child's underachievement based on birth order. "He's the middle child, what can I say?" According to Dr. James Dobson's research of thousands of parents, he found little evidence that temperament was influenced by birth order. Genetics played a more significant role. He did find a slight tendency for a compliant firstborn child to be followed by a strong-willed sibling. Of particular relevance to achievement, the compliant child is likely to be more socially well-adjusted as an adolescent than is the strong-willed child.

Divorce. Breakdown of the family is one of the most significant issues in America today. Divorce has become so common that we cannot overlook its impact on our nation's children. About half of marriages begun in the 70s are predicted to fail, and each divorce has been described as the death of a small civilization.

The strongest impact of divorce may be found in our schools. Across America, principals and teachers report dramatic increases in aggressive behavior by children from single-parent families. The effects of the emotional drama in their lives prevent them from seeing the importance of spelling tests and multiplication facts. Here are some of the findings and effects of divorce on children:

1. Divorce is not like a bad cold—acute discomfort, short recovery, then back on their feet with no residual harm.
2. Not all children suffer negative consequences from divorce.
3. Divorce is deceptive. Legally, it's one event; but in reality, it's a chain of events strung together throughout a child's life.
4. Children of divorce are twice as likely to drop out of high school; boys are at greater risk here, and also exhibit more aggressive behavior.
5. Thirty percent of two-parent elementary students are high achievers, compared with seventeen percent of single-parent students.
6. Parents in stepfamilies do not spend as much time with their children as intact families or even single parents.
7. Stepfamilies contribute less to children's college education.

For over one million kids a year, the divorce experience is a reality. The goal for us as parents is that we handle divorce in a way that preserves our children's self-esteem and emotional health, and in a way that also salvages their academic potential.

Remember that divorce itself only plays a small role in underachievement; it just reinforces an existing weakness. The child who is encouraged to immerse himself in his school work, friends, and extracurricular activities is more likely to experience a more healthy and speedy recovery.

The effect that divorce has on a child is in the hands of the parents. If parents allow it, kids certainly will lean on the my-parents-are-divorced crutch as an excuse for anything they don't want to do. Families split by divorce are urged to be consistent in parenting guidelines and to remain physically and emotionally involved in the youngsters' lives. Parental conflict is cited as the major cause of children's behavioral and academic problems, not the divorce itself.

One important point that parents can make to the million children a year affected by divorce is that they have a heavenly Father who will never abandon them and who is always there for them. They may feel they come from a dysfunctional family, but God is not a dysfunctional Father, and they need never be embarrassed if they are members of God's family. It's a choice of accepting a *damaged-model* mindset or a *challenged-model* one.

Self-Esteem Substitutes. A very-common denominator of underachievement and low self-esteem is the inappropriate use of time and talents. Parents of underachievers often allow extracurricular activities to act as substitutes for salvaging their child's plummeting self-esteem.

---

school achievement must be the child's priority focus in order for his self-esteem to reflect normal growth.

On the surface, this approach may appear to be a plausible one. But when scholastic achievement becomes secondary to sports, ballet, music lessons, scouts, etc., getting a student back on the academic track will be an up-hill battle!

When parents give credit to elective activities for what little self-esteem the child has, they're reluctant to take them away, fearing this would deliver another damaging blow to the child's self-esteem. The point of fact is that when the child is learning at a pace normal for his peer group, he begins to develop a positive self-image. That's why school achievement must be the child's priority focus in order for his self-esteem to reflect normal growth.

I've counseled many high-school clients who were capable of As and Bs, but were getting Ds and Fs. Their parents had tried restricting everything but the one thing that really mattered to them—sports! When I suggest that parents put sports on hold or at least require appropriate grades for this privilege, they begin to waffle! Parents think that they're taking away the only source of their child's self-worth. One parent even defended, "I'd be compromising the team if I pulled my child out. He's a key player." My reply, "Think about it, Dad. Without Babe Ruth, there's still baseball!"

Some Concluding Thoughts

Why do some children get involved with drugs, choose the wrong friends, or consider school a prolonged delay of their personal independence? Is it chance, better genes, environment? Are there some things that parents can do that will produce kids who can survive, despite circumstances that normally would suggest the opposite outcome?

Research has shown that children are resilient and able to survive in spite of adverse circumstances like poverty, abuse, and even drunken, ill, or disturbed parents when their environment includes the following: hobbies, friendships, responsibility, perseverance, stress preparedness, success experiences, continued learning, and optimism.

Traits of a healthy family include communication, shared meals, support, respect, trust, play, balanced interaction, shared leisure time, shared responsibility, sense of right and wrong, rituals and traditions, shared religion, privacy rights, service to others, and admittance of problems. All these traits are parallels for developing a healthy self-concept!

The most significant challenge for America's parents is to make sure that our children have the right combination of love, discipline, and direction that enables them to become whatever God intended. As parents, this is our primary responsibility.

Post View and What Parents Can Do

- Self-esteem is self-discovery of one's potential, character, and motives, and is perhaps the cornerstone of achievement.

- A healthy self-esteem begins with a belief in one's Creator.

- A self-esteem elixir cannot be bought!

- Self-esteem is *catching*, if parents are *carriers!*

- Parents who are *stretchers* and *reachers* make good *teachers!*

- Teach your child to avoid *stinkin' thinkin'!*

- Send your child off to school with a smile in his heart and positive thoughts for the day.

- Resolve to *re-ignite* your child's self-esteem *pilot light;*

    - Expect your child to perform at his potential
    - Give him *realistic compliments,* but avoid *inflated praise*
    - Eliminate her underachievement *crutches*
    - Limit his extracurricular activities
    - Communicate to her that *learning* is her primary responsibility!

- Enter your child's self-esteem level here _____.

4

Who's in the Driver's Seat?

"Inconsistency produces an oppositional child,
or at best a yo-yo;
first it's yes, then it's no."

ANONYMOUS

Raising Achievers is about parents taking back control of their child's education. My prerequisite for this chapter title was that it infer movement, because achievement, learning, responsibility, and self-motivation all imply action.

In this chapter, suggestions will be given for taking kids' potential and turning it into school success. Parents, when the issue is the achievement of your child, guess who's in the driver's seat?

Each of us has probably used the following saying: "You can lead a horse to water, but you can't make him drink." However, if

I were that very thirsty horse, and cool, refreshing water was only a gulp away, I wouldn't need a "giddyap" to head me in that direction! It's also true that we can send children to school, but we can't force them to learn. What parents must do is make them thirsty!

Then who really is in the driver's seat? The child is, and that's who it should be. However, parents write the driver's manual, issue the driver's permit, and determine the destination. Obviously, we're referring to kids who need to be pushed into gear, and about who does the pushing! As a teacher, let me share with you that most kids get a little "mushy" if parents aren't just a tad pushy!

Remedial Programs Revisited

Diane Ravitch, assistant secretary at the U.S. Department of Education, says that "high expectations, rigorous and challenging curriculum, and parent expectations" are recognized by educators to be the most critical factors in school achievement. She also cited "confidence building" as playing a key role, and one way teachers (and parents) can build "achievement hope" in kids is by telling them they can do anything.

There are some innovative programs testing these very ideas in acceleration schools across the country, and progress by these students has been phenomenal. What's interesting is that these programs did not involve advanced kids. In fact, 87 percent of the kids in these programs initially placed below the average for their grades on standardized tests! So, parents, if we expect performance and require it, we get it!

In light of this study and others, educators are beginning to take a second look at remedial instruction as a concept and at the techniques of remedial instruction in general. Traditional remedial programs often stigmatize remedial kids; and their education is often linked to boring, repetitive instruction in which they get further and further behind, according to Lamar Alexander, former U.S. Secretary of Education.

I couldn't agree more. From my experience, parents too often place an average-ability, underachieving child in one of these remedial school programs before considering the other alternatives —helping the child themselves or acquiring a qualified, private tutor.

Don't misunderstand me. All remedial school programs are not the same, and they're not all bad. But quality private assistance brings better and quicker results for the child. That's why trained parents make excellent tutors!

Para-Teachers (Parents as Tutors)

For the sake of our discussion on this topic, let's say you have a fifth grader reading at second-grade level and doing math at third-grade level. It's already been established that this child has at least average ability. As a wise parent you have a right to be concerned, and you're probably wondering where to go to get some private assistance. My question is this: Why not help him yourself? Interested parents can do most anything when it comes to helping their kids!

Don't be surprised if, at this point, you contract what I call "parent paralysis. First, you're unsure about your child's real ability; next, about what he needs to know; and last, about whether or not you're really the one to be helping him with his school work.

All that this "paralyzing thinking" does is prevent wary parents from setting appropriate, behavioral, grade-level, and overall achievement expectations for their children. This inaction really only serves to escalate the problems.

The prescription for parent paralysis is to become a para-teacher, a parent trained to tutor! We have paralegals trained to assist attorneys; why not para-teachers trained to help children. The operative word is *trained*. Because no one is as interested in your child's achievement as you are, you will be an excellent para-teacher.

Here are the qualifications you will need. (1) Know your child's achievement ability. (2) Know the basics of discipline. (3) Have confidence in the subject to be tutored. (4) Be able to work calmly and pleasantly with your child for fifteen to thirty minutes at a time! If you do lack confidence in the subject matter, or you lose control easily, it would be in the best interest of your child for you to find a qualified tutor.

With a little direction and some support materials available from your child's teacher, you can become an excellent tutor. When I'm working with young clients, I have parents sit in on the first couple of sessions so they can learn a few tutorial techniques and guidelines to use at home. This practice has proven very beneficial, and the child progresses much more rapidly when the parent knows how to work tutorially with the child.

The answers to some of the questions I'm frequently asked by parents of underachievers may be helpful to some potential para-teachers.

1. Why doesn't my child like school? Probably because expectations are made of him there!

2. Does my child have a learning disability? It's unlikely. Chances are 90-95 percent against it. If you are really concerned, have her tested.

3. How can I get my child to do his homework? By stating that homework is not an option and is non-negotiable. Select appropriate consequences that ensure he does his homework. See also chapter 7, "Homework Without the (Parents') Hassle."

4. How much should I help with homework? As much as you could if you were out of the country most of the time! Ideally, the homework tether should be cut by the end of third grade, and your job should be one of seeing that homework is done and that needed materials are provided. Dictating spelling words, using math flash cards, etc., are acceptable exceptions.

5. When should she develop responsibility? From approximately three years of age, she should be learning to develop responsibility through age-appropriate chores, such as being responsible for inventorying the soap and toilet tissue in the bathrooms!

6. How can I get him to be more organized? By setting reasonable organizational standards (with back-up consequences for failing to meet these standards) in such areas as his room, closet, drawers, toys, games, desk, notebook, and school work assignments.

7. How do I know what she is capable of doing? See answer to question 2. If professional testing is indicated, consult her teacher or principal for referrals.

8. How can I get him to do what I know he can do? By remembering that all behavior is maintained by its consequences. Find out what he likes most, then reward him once he's reached his behavioral and/or achievement objectives.

Let me qualify my answer to question 4, concerning how much homework help should be given to a child. As the answer states, the ideal is that children be responsible for their own homework beginning at fourth-grade level. That's the ideal, but reality may demand modification. What do you do with a child who is achieving two to three grades below grade level? You do whatever it takes to bring him up to grade level. Start with reading, then math, since these two subjects are foundational to all subsequent learning. Use good judgment here. You may elect to hire a tutor, or you may decide to become his para-teacher. Once the problem is resolved, and from that point forward, he's on his own.

Traffic-Light Parents

Too many parents are what I call "traffic-light parents." First it's STOP, then it's GO! Or, first it's YES, then it's NO! We need to set expectations, assign responsibilities, and design consequences that get results. In my experience over some thirty years working with parents of underachievers, most scenarios continue to present two common elements: parents are simply afraid to set appropriate expectations for their children, and they are inconsistent in their discipline. The discipline code you select must include efficient, consistent, and corrective methods that change the child's pattern of underachievement and behavior.

Too many parents are what
I call "traffic-light parents."
First it's STOP,
then it's GO!

Our intentions are good, and our attitudes surrounding child-rearing philosophy are on track. The only thing wrong is that good intentions, attitudes, and philosophies are all passive entities. On the other hand, setting goals, disciplinary strategies, and designing consequences require action. My task is mostly one of giving parents my professional permission to move from the philosophical mode into the consistent action mode, where achievement and productivity happen.

"Real" Discipline

For a quick review of how the word discipline is defined, I went to *Webster's New World Dictionary.* Discipline is a "branch of knowledge or learning; *training* that develops *self-control, charac-ter, orderliness* and *efficiency;* strict control to enforce *obedience;* self-control or *orderly conduct;* acceptance of or *submission* to *authority* and control; a system of *rules,* as for the conduct of members of a monastic order; *treatment* that *corrects* or punishes." Reads like a description of a drill sergeant, doesn't it? Remember, someone must be in control. And if parents don't take control, their kids will!

Every parent knows that children can be both wonderful and a little wicked at the same time. Each child is definitely a unique creation of God, wonderfully designed, with enormous potential and interests. But *willfulness* and *won'tfulness* surface early on, and the child can turn *wicked* very quickly if allowed to develop without proper guidance and limits.

The italicized words used in Webster's definition are the key elements of discipline that parents must master if they want the student back in the driver's seat of achievement. Let's examine Webster's components of discipline as they relate specifically to achievement. Make sure these are in your child's drivers' manual.

Training, Self-Control, and Character

In chapter 3 on self-esteem, we already discussed how answering to God could influence the development of a more healthy self-esteem, respect for learning, and self-reliance. Behavior codes that theoretically contradict that of God's presume a greater wisdom. I'm neither that presumptuous, nor do I wish to dictate the personal discipline code that you practice with your child. What I am saying is that discipline guidelines are necessary in order to "re-energize" a reluctant learner. So, whatever code of "shalts" and "shalt nots" that you select, follow it consistently and with gusto!

Without guidelines that set rules of conduct and behavior of people, there would be chaos. And for those who choose to deviate from the rules, there must also be consequences for missing the mark. Without some standards of acceptable, expectable behavior, parents need not anticipate accountability.

Most of the widely accepted values, codes of behavior, and discipline guidelines in America originated from the Bible and a belief in God. These include those which refer to child rearing in particular. Even our judicial system requires witnesses to swear "to tell the truth, the whole truth, so help me God."

However, during the seventies, many of these revered precepts and long-held beliefs about child rearing and discipline became subjects for popular debate. In this new era, *spanking* was out, and *time out* was in. Parent respect was suspect, and obedience to authority was all but abolished. Today, parents who administer corporal punishment can find themselves charged with child abuse.

Yale law professor Stephen Carter, in his book *The Culture of Disbelief,* charges that liberal elites "have come to belittle religious devotion, to humiliate believers, and . . . to discourage religion as a serious activity." Secular humanists appear to be following a systematic plan for blotting out religion from our public life. Since the Supreme Court pronounced the final "Amen" to school prayer in 1962, look what has happened: Violent crime has increased from 16.1 per 10,000 to 75.8. The illegitimacy rate has soared from 5.3 percent to 28 percent.

No more Christmas carols, nativity scenes, prayers at graduation or sports events are allowed. References to this nation's religious origins are disappearing as fast as new history texts can be printed. Kids are no longer able to get the guidance they need from our public schools, the media, or from "popular" culture.

Am I totally out of touch, or is there possibly a correlation between the mayhem and madness in our society and the low-level expectations, authority, and discipline? No, God's admonition to parents to "bring up a child in the way he should go" was not condoning child abuse. Rather He was assigning parents the role of caring enough to love, discipline, manage, and monitor their children.

Based upon the Bible and the millions who believe that its teachings have serious merit, I've selected a few discipline-related quotes for quick reference.

> "No discipline seems pleasant at the time, but painful. Later on, however, it produces a harvest of righteousness and peace for those who have been trained by it." (Heb. 12:11, NIV).

> "The rod and correction imparts wisdom, but a child left to himself disgraces his mother." (Prov. 29:15, NIV).

> "A foolish son is a grief to his father, and bitterness to her who bore him" (Prov. 17:25, NASB).

> "A foolish son is the calamity of his father" (Prov. 19:13).

> "Train up a child in the way he should go: and when he is old, he will not depart from it" (Prov. 22:6).

"Foolishness is bound in the heart of a child, but the rod of correction shall drive it far from him" (Prov. 22:15).

"He who spares the rod hates his son, but he who loves him is careful to discipline him" (Prov. 13:24, NIV).

"Children, obey your parents in the Lord" (Eph. 6:1).

"Do not withhold discipline from a child, if you punish him with the rod, he will not die. Punish him with the rod, and save his soul from death" (Prov. 23:13–14, NIV).

One way to build character in a child is through training and self-control. Even though it is an ongoing task, it is not complex. Former U.S. Secretary of Education, Lamar Alexander, says if we are to improve America's schools, it will have to be done at the community-by-community level, starting with our own children. He asks parents these questions: "Have you spent fifteen minutes in a conversation with your child today (the national average)? Read to the child? Discussed right and wrong and religion? Played together? Gone somewhere together? Listened? Hugged? Checked on homework? School attendance? Monitored (and limited) TV watching?"

According to Webster, discipline provides the training that develops self-control and character. Yet, many parents report feelings of inadequacy when it comes to discipline. In order for you to raise achievers, you simply must gain at least moderate proficiency in Discipline 101. The basic guidelines are in this chapter, with additional help in chapters 5 and 7.

If you are the parent of more than one child, you're already aware that the same discipline may not work as effectively with every child. Parents must decide for themselves what their specific do's and don'ts will be, so long as the code selected contains those basic elements of Webster's definition given earlier.

Authority, Control, and Obedience

Teachers, especially new ones, also can have problems disciplining, as I learned on my first teaching assignment. I followed

61

eleven substitutes who had refused to return to this particular school a second day because of the discipline problems within the P.E. class of sixty girls! To my surprise (and the principal's), I had little difficulty controlling the class, even though I knew nothing about teaching volleyball. As a single parent, I guess I had learned quickly about the basics of discipline and crowd control in order to survive!

Confident parents definitely have
an edge in parenting achievers.

The most effective teachers and parents are confident disciplinarians. Confident parents definitely have an edge in parenting achievers. Some of these confidence areas require both teachers and parents to assume a position of authority; show honesty, fairness, and a sense of humor; establish behavioral standards, and be consistent; post consequences of inappropriate behavior.

A mother came to my office bringing her daughter, Karen, who appeared to be a normal, healthy, and intelligent little girl. She was referred to me by her last school. In fact, for the past two years, Karen had attended three private schools, none of which had extended her an invitation to return to their school the following year. This was based in part on her poor achievement, but mostly because of her behavior problems. And Karen was only six years old!

The fact that she didn't get along with her classmates came as no surprise, because she didn't get along well at home either, according to her mother. One example of her inappropriate behavior occurred at McDonald's. Evidently, their Happy Meal did not live up to its name for Karen, for she demanded a Ronald McDonald puppet also. As Karen's mother explained to her that she hadn't brought along enough money to purchase both a Happy Meal and a puppet, Karen landed a swift kick to her mother's shin!

You say, "I thought we were talking about school achievement." You're right, but behavior, discipline, and achievement begin in the home. What kids get away with at home, continues in the classroom. And when kids with problems like Karen's fail to get teachers with good disciplinary skills, too often they follow the *underdisciplined* path to *underachievement*.

Test your own discipline proficiency level with this incident at McDonald's.

TEST 1. Circle what you would do, if Karen were your child.

  A. Kick her back, and give her a swat on the bottom!

  B. Leave the Happy Meal at McDonalds, and without saying a word, take Karen by the hand and head for the nearest exit.

  C. Take the Happy Meal and lecture her on the spot about the rudeness of kicking.

  D. Take the Happy Meal and escort Karen to the car.

  E. Blush, apologize for your poverty, and promise to get a second job so you can fulfill her every future wish.

Let's analyze the options. A. This is probably the impulse choice, and it's likely we've all succumbed a few times. B. This option is probably the best of those listed, but needs some follow-up. C. Absolutely not. D. She definitely should not get the Happy Meal after this incident. E. Obviously, this option is ludicrous.

Her mother shared with me another example of Karen's noncompliant behavior. Getting her dressed for school everyday promised heated confrontations. She refused to wear almost every dress her mother selected, simply because she didn't like them. "That's ugly, weird; it's a yucky color; nobody wears stuff like this." The clothing either had the wrong label, or wasn't currently being worn by the latest pop stars.

Here's another opportunity for you to hone your disciplinary prowess with our six-year-old clothing critic.

TEST 2. How would you handle Karen's behavior?

A. Try to educate her choice in clothes.

B. Plead with her to wear the clothes because you've already spent good money on them.

C. Demand she wear them because you said so.

D. Give some of her clothes away, and for any future purchases, she is allowed to choose only from the items you have pre-approved!

E. Teach her how lucky she is by taking her with you to distribute some of her clothes to needy children.

Let's analyze the options. A. For a six-year-old, this option will be of little help. B. Immaturity precludes benefit from a lesson in economics. C. This is a possibility, but rigid and less productive, long-term. D. This is not a bad second choice. E. This is the best option offered, but would be even better if combined with D.

The results of Karen's testing indicated that her learning system was intact. Her attitude was the primary problem, and it was in need of major adjustment, if not a complete overhaul! Remember, kids do whatever parents tolerate, and by her own admission, Karen's mom feared she would lose her child's love if she disciplined her.

According to John Rosemond, parental authority must be clearly in place before potential for affection within the parent-child relationship can be released. Karen's mother lacked the parenting confidence that would have allowed her to exercise the authority needed to bring about change in Karen's attitude.

I challenge you to put parental authority to the test. Once you begin to exercise your authority position with love and maturity, you will see an immediate difference in your child's attitudes, respect, and obedience. It is very important for parents to present a united front in regard to behavior and achievement expectations. Kids need to know what the ground rules, guidelines, expectations, and consequences are. If your kids see that the two of you are not in agreement, you can count on the fact that they will play "divide and conquer," pitting one against the other.

I don't know what happened with Karen. I never saw her again, because her mother was afraid to follow my suggestions for discipline. Psychologists, academic therapists, and teachers have limitations that parents don't have. Only parents have the authority to discipline and set consequences that gets kids to apply the instruction from the classroom which then enables them to achieve. The protocol should follow this sequence: Parents expect. Teachers teach. Kids learn!

Kids need to know what the ground rules, guidelines, expectations, and consequences are.

Sometimes my job is one of getting parents to accept the fact that they've spoiled their children rotten! Fred Gosman has some funny, practical, and terse pointers for those who have. He was so strongly convinced that kids were out of control, pampered, and spoiled, that he wrote the book entitled *Spoiled Rotten*. Gosman recommends using a reasonable consequence instead of giving kids a seventh chance. When you have a child with a "porcupine and prickly-pear personality," it's past discussion time. And don't say you can't get your child to *move*, until you read about the rabbit.

An overindulgent rabbit was stuck in a hole after eating too much. The rabbit beckoned a frog who happened by to help him get out of the hole. While the friendly frog went to fetch a ladder to help the rabbit out of the hole, a snake appeared at the other end of the hole, and guess what? The stuck rabbit suddenly was able to extricate himself from the hole! Sometimes parents have to assume the role of the snake in order to roust kids from their underachieving ruts.

65

Orderliness, Organization, and Efficiency

I'm reminded of Tony, a client living with his grandmother. Tony was an intelligent twelve-year-old; but he also was a surly, disobedient, and rather obnoxious preteen approaching puberty. During a casual conversation at the beginning of one his sessions, he boasted that he had an expensive skateboard that cost over a hundred dollars! I asked him how he acquired such an expensive skateboard, and his cocky reply was, "I bought it with my own money."

Later, in a private meeting with his grandmother, I queried what criteria, if any, she used for giving Tony an allowance. In light of his D-F effort in all core subject areas, I couldn't imagine why she would give this child an allowance. From Grandma, I learned that his allowance had no levy. As long as he had a branch on the family tree and his eyes remained blue, he apparently satisfied allowance entitlement!

Aside from a bad attitude, Tony's main problem was disorganization aggravated by an inconsistent pattern of homework study time. On the rare occasions when Tony bothered to do his homework, he frequently lost it before its due date. For starters, his notebook was the epitome of disorganization—a classic three-ring "litter binder"!

One of my requirements of clients is that they keep a neat notebook, including organizers for each subject. Returned and corrected homework and tests are each to be placed behind their own separate organizers, sequenced by date. No ripped-out papers allowed, and no papers showing outside the edges of the notebook binder. If I can grasp a notebook by its spine and give it a firm shake, and papers fall out, this is not an organized notebook!

Parents, most teachers grade and return homework and tests within three days to a week. The student should then correct all errors and file them behind the proper organizers in his notebook. If this procedure is followed, these corrected tests and assignments become excellent study guides for future tests.

The grandmother followed my advice and gave Tony the appropriate "snake" push. She temporarily confiscated his prized skateboard; the allowance ceased; a daily home-study time was set and followed; his notebook usually passed most unannounced "shake tests"; and Tony got his "achievement act" together. We all came out winners! His teacher and grandmother think I'm a miracle worker! Really, the only thing that I did was to identify the problem and outline the steps for change in Tony's behavior and achievement. It was Grandma who saw to it that Tony took the steps.

Let me give you another example. Fourteen-year-old Ashley, a young lady with an "attitude," was referred to me for homework and school detention problems. I quickly learned why Ashley was getting frequent detentions. For example, her teacher gave her detention on one occasion for slamming her books down on the desk as she reached her seat only seconds before the tardy bell rang. Her timing was such that the teacher knew it was an obvious attention-getting act. And this was not Ashley's first attention-getting tactic.

On the same day she received detention for the book-slamming incident, Ashley arrived for our session, still carrying her anger baggage. She was mumbling remarks, like "I never have any free time; I hate school, hate the teacher." Ashley made no attempt to follow our session routine—getting homework out and beginning immediately. Instead, after taking her seat, she just stared down, obviously wanting me to notice her. When I acknowledged her inaction, she continued to sit, sending "eye-hate" messages. Finally I said, "Okay, Ashley, it looks as if this is not going to be a productive session. Because I don't charge parents for sessions when nothing is accomplished, I'd like you to phone your mother and have her come pick you up. Tell her that you've chosen not to do anything productive in our session today." Without missing a beat, she took out her books and began her homework. She wasn't about to give her mother this message! Remember, "when you expect, you get; when you don't expect, you get disrespect!"

Authority vs. Authoritarian

Once parents have established a firm and loving relationship with their kids and have let them know what they expect of them, kids usually obey. These expectations must be reasonable, and kids must know that you will follow through with the necessary consequences—consistently!

However, rules without that relationship beg for rebellion. There is a fine line of difference between *authority* and *authoritarian*. The difference is that *relationship* is missing in *authoritarian*, and it is present in *authority*. Homes are not democracies; parents always cast a "weighted" vote. Although your role may seem like that of a benevolent monarch, keep in mind that there must be an authority figure in the home, somewhere for the "buck" to stop. If parents relinquish their control, kids will take control.

All kids will resist authority, starting at about age two! Don't expect your kids to thank you for the privilege of taking out the garbage or cleaning up their messy rooms. They're going to procrastinate, argue, and claim that you're the only parent on the planet who even assigns chores!

It's natural for kids to argue and talk back, according to Dr. Kevin Leman. Recognize it as buying time and trying to wear you down. However, it takes only two phrases: *nevertheless* or *regardless,* followed by, *do it now!*

If they continue pressuring you with their immature eloquence, hand them a tape recorder and a tape. Tell them they can continue to "pontificate for perpetuity," but not in your presence. Promise to listen later when both of you have had time to calm down. That way, they get to tell their side—that is, if they actually bother to record their thoughts. I'm not convinced that kids want you to hear their side as much as they want to delay doing what you've asked of them. Some kids just like to watch you turn red, see the blood vessels pop out in your face and neck, and see you lose your cool! But, at least, they can't say you refused to listen to them. You've only exercised your parental authority and the right to choose the time you will listen.

Danger Anger

Let me say just a word about anger. Although occasional parent anger is inevitable and common, watch that your anger doesn't dip into the danger level. I'm talking about anger that can lead to a child's loss of respect for you and, subsequently, maybe even the motivation to achieve. Try a little cleverness and wit, instead. These two go a long way toward deflecting the anger and reducing your blood pressure!

One writer suggested that parents fund a "forgiveness account" for unresolved anger. I think this idea has some merit, especially for the younger child. When Billy occasionally steps out of an achieving mode, instead of getting angry, make a forgiveness withdrawal. But after you make the appropriate allowances for his immaturity, firmly restate his behavioral expectations. Remember, learning is a life-long journey. Make it as enjoyable as possible for your child. Love him and enjoy him as he grows, learns, and matures. Good parenting mandates that we strive for the right balance between authority and authoritarian.

Post View and What Parents Can Do

- "Traffic-Light Parents" are afraid to set academic expectations for their children and are inconsistent in their discipline.

- Put your child back in the "driver's seat" for learning, but remember that you are the one who issues his driving permit and destination guidelines.

- Verify your child's performance ability as the first step in planning her achievement process.

- Increase your parenting confidence skills, which give you an edge in parenting an achiever.

- Select a discipline code and consequences that correct and provide training in developing your child's self-control and character.

- A well-planned discipline code and consequences will re-energize your reluctant learner. If the behavior isn't changing, the consequences need tightening.

- A united front by both parents, regarding discipline, grades, behavior, and consequences precludes "divide and conquer" attempts by the child.

- All achievement expectations for an underachiever contain two elements: something to stop and start.

- Use these two-phrase argument deflectors frequently: *nevertheless* or *regardless,* followed by *do it now.*

- Select three priority behavioral and grade expectations for your child and list them here.

Behavioral Expectations

Remember that all behavioral change must include something to *start* and something to *stop*. Either is appropriate for your list below.

1. _____

2. _____

3. _____

Grade Expectations

Make sure that your expectations are realistic, then require that he works at his ability. Grades should be projected for each specific school subject.

1. _____

2. _____

3. _____

PART TWO

Turning Potential into Achievement

5

When It's Time to Put the Rudder in the Water!

"Many of life's failures are people who did not realize how close they were to success when they gave up."

—THOMAS EDISON

*I*n John Rogers' and Peter Williams' best selling book, *Do It,* there's a marvelous statement about achievement that sets the tone for Part 2 and is particularly relevant to this chapter: "It's not obtaining the goal, but what we learn about ourselves along the way." In order to realize our dreams, the co-authors said we must be "focused, disciplined, persevering, caring, worthy, excited, enthusiastic, and passionate." What kids learn about themselves during the achievement process, they can take with them throughout their lives. The quest for parents is to make learning an adventure for their kids.

I hope you're at least in general agreement with most of the philosophical and theoretical causes and problems of under-achievement as presented in Part 1. I assume that you've responded to the parent-action areas in the Post View and What Parents Can Do sections at the end of chapters 1 through 4.

- *Chapter 1:* You verified your child's performance ability, are in the process of eliminating his "Behavior Deadlies," and have selected a consistent behavior code.

- *Chapter 2:* You checked out your "Parenting Quotient" and made the appropriate steps to improve your parenting skills.

- *Chapter 3:* You measured the self-esteem level of your child and made some mental notes on how to re-ignite his or her self-image.

- *Chapter 4:* You selected some behavioral and grade expectations for your child and resolved to put him in the driver's seat with achievement as his destination.

These are all necessary steps that need to be firmly in place (or at least in process) prior to embarking on part 2, where we'll be taking Billy and Susie's potential and turning it into achievement!

Capables and Electables

"Why can't you just love me the way I am?" the child asked. "I do, son, so much that I can't allow you to do less than your best," replied his father.

It's time to set your child's achievement goals. The last thing that parents need is worry about whether or not they're pushing the child beyond her ability. So, as we suggested in part 1, have your child tested if there is any doubt about her achievement potential.

Request a consultation with your child's teacher to ask about her ability and learning needs. Teachers are not only trained professionals, they also see your child over a long period of time, observing her on her good and bad days. They are in a unique position to provide an objective evaluation of her effort and ability in relation to her achievement. Let's agree that the child's *capables* should become his *expectables*. Stop worrying about ruffling your child's feathers. Your new parenting confidence tells you that the child is headed in the wrong direction, and *it's time to put the rudder in the water*. As the rudder of a ship gives direction to the vessel, so will wise parents provide the child's achievement direction and guidelines.

Consider the following Weis Truism that took form after studying achievement in a 30-year, 35,000-student laboratory setting as a parent and educator: "Kids prefer to do things their own way, in their own time, and given the option, may do nothing!"

In fact, many kids think their mission on earth is to have fun. Just remember your child is sitting in a classroom with approximately thirty others of the same age. How would you like to have thirty six-year-olds or twelve-year-olds all day long? Think about it. That's why it's so important to send well-disciplined kids to school with attitudes to learn, if we want them to have the most achievement advantages possible.

Naming, Blaming, and Retraining

If we could give kids an achievement template and ask them to fill it, wouldn't that be great? Or if they were remote controlled, we could just push their achievement button and select a 4.0 GPA. Unfortunately, this isn't the case. So the choice we're left with is steering kids in the right direction.

We identify and give a name to the problems and causes that prevent kids from reaching their potential. Problems need a *handle* for convenience in discussing them with the child. The three grade and behavioral expectations that you listed at the end of chapter 4 as the priority problems in your child's underachievement will be the focus of this chapter.

In chapter 1, I provided a pretty comprehensive list gathered by educators of causes or problems in underachievement. For convenience, they're briefly restated here.

- Poor Attitude
- No Perseverance
- Absenteeism
- Homework Problems Over Commitment
- Underdisciplined/Undermotivated
- Tired
- Lazy
- Poor Nutrition
- Over-indulgent Parents
- Under/Overprojected Ability
- Retention vs. Tutorial

All of these are within the parent's ball park! The "experts" have had their chance at solving the problems in education. Parents, it's your turn.

Loving parents have a tendency to shield their children from every problem and to rescue them from every unpleasant situation. But "slaying all your kids' dragons" does not prepare them for the real world. They learn through perseverance and small successes how to confront and solve their own problems, overcome daily obstacles, and resolve conflicts by themselves. This same perseverance and sense of accomplishment also increase self-esteem and strength of character.

Parent Denial Statements

You say, "But I don't think I'm really an overindulgent parent." It's possible that you're just not unaware of it. Here are some denial statements frequently made by parents who innocently may be guilty of contributing to their child's underachievement.

- There must be a mistake; my child doesn't lie.
- My child told me you never give homework.
- That's strange, he never acts this way at home.
- No other teacher has had this problem with her.
- Maybe my child is bored.
- I saw him do his homework.

- The problem is that other kids pick on her.
- He's just a boy. He'll grow out of it; I did.

Underachiever Behavior Clues

I don't think I've ever encountered an underachiever without some behavior clues. Watch out for these clues.

- Refuses to do homework.
- Fails to bring homework materials home.
- Makes numerous careless mistakes in homework.
- Demonstrates poor effort in doing homework.
- Fails to complete homework.
- Feigns ignorance of how to do homework.
- Lies about having any homework to do.
- Loses homework after it is done.
- "Forgets" to study for tests.
- Fails to take notes to study from.
- Fails to allow adequate homework-completion time.
- Reports headaches, stomachaches at homework time.

If you want your child to be an achiever, develop the skill of restraint in providing too much help with homework. Most underachievers have shielding, overprotecting, "dragon-slaying" parents, those who make far too many decisions for the child that she could've made for herself. This is not good. What we end up producing is selfish, self-indulgent, stubborn kids. Over-indulgence not only weakens a child, but also diminishes his learning capacity, initiative, and resourcefulness.

Are you ready to take the naming and blaming step in solving your child's underachievement? Here's my suggestion. Parents go out for a nice dinner without the kids. Enjoy your dinner, but during the course of the evening, cut to the real objective—designing a plan of achievement for your child.

Resolve any points of disagreement regarding grade expectations, their extracurricular activities, and even the consequences that will be used. All of these must be part of this plan. The final step of the evening is for both of you to agree to love your child vigorously and to support the plan consistently.

You might even take an enlarged rendering of my typical Achievement-Planning Worksheet that follows. This way you can actually complete it in this pleasant atmosphere. If you've been doing your end-of-the-chapter homework, you already have the information written out. At the end of chapter 1, you listed your child's underachievement problems. At the end of chapter 4, you listed three grade and behavioral expectations. Use these as your child's objectives. Aren't you glad you did your homework?

Overindulgence not only weakens a child, but also diminishes his learning capacity, initiative, and resourcefulness.

In the first column, list each problem, in priority order. In the second column, list the expectations or objectives. Then decide on a few logical steps your child needs to take in order to reach each objective. The next column is for the projected timeline for him to reach each objective. In the last column, list the selected consequences to be used when he does not meet his objectives.

If all these elements are not a part of the change agenda, do not expect significant change to occur!

Family Meeting

The last step is retraining. For this step, you'll want to call a family meeting. Only the parents and the underachieving child participate in this meeting.

Once the Achievement-Planning Worksheet is filled in, it needs to be formally presented to the child. When you expect to implement change with kids, it's a good idea to make it just a tad

Achievement-Planning Worksheet

Problem	Objective	Steps	Timeline	Consequences
1.	1.	1.		
		2.		
		3.		
2.	2.	1.		
		2.		
		3.		
3.	3.	1.		
		2.		
		3.		

of a "production" to emphasize the importance of the new plan. Never go into a family meeting without an agenda to keep you focused. Poorly-defined problems and "fuzzy" objectives produce poor results. So plan ahead of time the specific points to be discussed with your child. Remember, the focus is diffused when aimed in too many directions, so focus on those three change areas listed at the end of chapter 4.

Prior to setting up this meeting, you'll need to plan your agenda. If you want your child to view his achievement as an adventure, use some creativity and imagination in getting this process off the ground. For fun, you might mail him an invitation to the meeting, with the note, "Refreshments will be served!" The formality of an invitation adds to the intrigue and importance of the meeting. By the way, do not include a copy of the agenda. That would ruin the suspense factor.

The more thought and planning that go into this meeting, the better response you can expect from the child. Be sure that the agenda includes, at least, the following items:

- Meeting Time, Place, Date
- Purpose of Meeting
- Problems Stated
- Child's Achievement Plan
- 3 Behavioral Objectives & 3 Grade Objectives (See chap. 4, last page.)
- Steps to Reach Each Objective
- Timeline
- Consequences for Unmet Objectives

The achievement plan is ready, and his invitation is in the mail. The day has arrived for the family meeting. This is an example of how your conversation might begin:

"I'm sure you're wondering what this meeting is all about. First, we both want to say that we love you very much. We think you're pretty neat in most ways. However, your teachers have told us that you're capable of doing quality work. According to information we've been given, you could be an A [or '__'] student.

Since we both feel that you have a lot of potential that you're not using, we're going to discuss your new plan of achievement. We've selected some problem areas that we're going to focus on together that will make your school work go more smoothly and, at the same time, improve your grades. Here's the plan. . . ."

Try not to use argumentative or derogatory statements. Some of these phrases may need some vocabulary adjustments, depending on your child's age.

Good and Bad Teachers

In the retraining process of the child's achievement, we can't ignore one critical area, his teachers. One of the most awesome responsibilities parents have is monitoring the quality of those who will direct their children's thoughts, ideas, and information system for approximately thirteen thousand hours from first through twelfth grade. These are their early, most impressionable, and formative years; and there's no second chance at these twelve years. So, it's obvious that parents will want to make sure their children get their fair share of good teachers. Good teachers are not only competent in their subject matter, confident and fair disciplinarians, experienced, and pleasant; they also like kids!

Having been a teacher, I certainly have known some teachers I would not have wanted for my children. And even though it may not be easy, or possible, to switch teachers once your child is assigned to a class, I urge you to make sure that at least he doesn't get two bad ones in a row.

Meet his teachers; attend all his parent-teacher conferences; and if you suspect trouble, take a day off from work to visit his class for a day. Show your child and his teachers that you're an interested and concerned parent.

In defense of the teacher's perspective, I've also placed an equal degree of responsibility upon parents for sending teachers respectful, well-disciplined kids with an attitude to learn. And I've asked that parents support teachers' classroom discipline and homework assignments to the letter. I believe my perspectives are balanced.

Objectives, Rewards, and Consequences

Objectives

A goal is the end result of having met one's objectives. A Yale study showed that the top 3 percent of successful people write down their daily goals! Your child's ultimate goal is to achieve his potential. Objectives are like arrows headed for targets. As you direct your child's achievement process, you'll be using a quiver full of them. You'll catch on quickly how to word them specifically so your child doesn't find a crack to crawl through.

Objectives must include these components: *who* is going to do *specifically what* by *when*, measured by *what proof.* Here are examples of the right and wrong wording of objectives.

Right Objective. Billy will bring his math grade up to a B by his next report card. Proof: his report card grade.

Wrong Objective. Billy will try harder in math. Proof: Billy will think he's doing better.

It's pretty obvious what's wrong with the second example. Note the fuzzy or intangible wording. Better could mean that his F moves to a D-. This is not exactly a giant step in effort or achievement for Billy, but he met the fuzzy objective!

The grade expectations that you establish for your child must specify that he maintain a certain quality in homework assignments as well as punctuality in meeting assignment deadlines. Don't just say, "Do better." Actually specify what, when, and method of proof in his objectives.

Rewards

We touched briefly on rewards in our discussion of inflated and realistic praise and compliments. Let me share with you some additional facts about rewards that I've learned from my experience and research.

Most psychologists and educators support using at least two categories of rewards with kids—tangible (visible) and intangible (invisible). Use of contingent (conditional) rewards is less desirable.

Tangible & Intangible Rewards. Both tangible and intangible rewards reinforce behavior and encourage performance that is expected and anticipated, *not* that which is a result of the child's choice. These types of rewards always have an element of *when,* not *if.* Add a timeline to these rewards; and when the specific behavior occurs, *voila,* present him the reward!

Contingent Rewards. Contingent rewards, on the other hand, always have an element of *if,* which indicates the child has a choice of whether or not to pursue an objective. Remember, reasonable objectives are not optional for the child. Too often, parents offer giant rewards for baby steps. For example, "If you get 100 percent on your spelling test this Friday, I'll do all your chores next week."

It doesn't take a genius to figure out how little Billy and Susie can use poor effort to their advantage in the future! So briefly stated: Stop with the *if's* and go with the *when's.* Here are some pointers about rewards that I've collected over the years. You may find them useful.

1. The best rewards are given as surprises.
2. Reward success toward a goal, not only the ultimate goal.
3. Reward mature progress in the appreciation of learning.
4. Avoid using contingent rewards, such as, "If you'll do thus and such, then I'll give you this and that."
5. Reward the behavior you want repeated.
6. Reward, minimally. Don't use money if a treat will do; don't use a treat if praise satisfies.
7. Use larger rewards to launch new objectives.
8. Reduce frequency of rewards after the early stages of performance.
9. Use lots of these: "Great!" "Good job!" "Wow!"
10. Recognize and compliment him in front of others.

11. Post examples of good school work.
12. Listen to him brag about an achievement.

Surprise Rewards. Surprise rewards are the best, and they can benefit the whole family. You give tokens (chips, marbles, etc.) for realistic progress toward his objectives, kindness, thoughtfulness, resourcefulness, good manners, good deeds, and anything else that is worthy of recognition throughout the week. At the end of the week, these accumulated tokens may be exchanged for a surprise.

These surprise rewards can be things you might already have been planning. Susie doesn't know that! A picnic at the park or beach, rental of a video, a trip to the arcade with Dad, making pizza, or baking cookies together, eating out, a family bike ride, etc., are all wonderful rewards to a kid. They are great self-esteem enhancers too, because your child earned them!

Consequences

But then we must talk about those who are not ready for rewards. If talking hasn't brought results, it's time for consequences.

Because you're a loving, interested parent, you've already developed the "relationship role" with your child. You've clearly defined behavioral boundaries and grade expectations. So, if Billy's not moving toward his goals yet, can you guess what's missing? Consequences! Remember, you are the only one with the authority to exact just the right consequences that will turn your child's potential into success.

Homes cannot function realistically as pure democracies, and homes as autocracies or dictatorships are equally undesirable. The ideal home operates as a quasi-democracy under the direction of benevolent authorities (not authoritarians). We need to give our children the "gift of loving limits, because failure to discipline is actually a form of child abuse. Kids don't act like it, but they really do appreciate loving parents who are also strict." Move this Weis Truism to the front burner: "Kids respect strength and mock weakness." Want proof? Take a look at some of their heroes: Clint Eastwood, Arnold Schwarzenegger, The American Gladiators,

Power Rangers, Captain Planet, Sylvester Stallone, Steven Seagal and whoever else happens to be the "Hero Contempo!"

After you've presented Billy with his achievement plan at the family meeting, expect and allow him to react. It's important that you listen to his defense of himself, because the listening has some face-saving benefit for him. After the listening, however, your response will be a calm, resolute "Nevertheless (or Regardless), starting now, this is what we expect of you." (Specify grades, behavior changes, attitudes, etc.) No argument, explaining, or further discussion. If they begin to squirm, contend, protest, and defend further, select some such comment as "That was then; this is now."

Here are some key points about consequences related to achievement that I include at my parent workshops. Review these as you compile your own list of consequences.

1. All behavior is maintained by its consequences.
2. Reality discipline includes consequences.
3. Parents must not be in competition for "Most Popular Parent."
4. The most effective achievement plan includes the best arsenal of consequences—clever, well-planned, and posted ones!
5. Consistency and immediacy are prerequisites for successful use of consequences.
6. Consequences should fit the infraction.
7. Consequences must focus on taking away what has meaning for the child—what he treasures most!
8. Don't take your child's underachievement personally. Kids lose respect for parents who preach, pout, and plead for understanding of how badly they're making us feel by their underachievement!

Parents' Power Areas

Let's say you've followed consistently all the suggestions and guidelines provided so far in *Raising Achievers,* and your child is still testing your authority and confidence as a parent. That's when it's time to "hit 'em where it hurts," and it couldn't be more appropriate than when it comes to imposing consequences! I suggest the following areas be included in your arsenal of consequences.

The Pocketbook. Kids' allowances are not entitlements! They should be put on hold until ability performance is a reality.

The Stomach. Make goodies, snacks, and desserts scarce to nonexistent. When the family eats out, Billy and Susie stay home with a sitter. Bread and water and solitary confinement have been found to effectively modify the behavior of hardened criminals in days gone by. Don't deny the potential effectiveness of restricting selected foods on your child's behavior!

The Social Calendar. Limit access to peers through the telephone, birthday celebrations, skating, school parties, summer camp, movies, arcade visits, etc. Putting these on hold assures you have their attention!

Sports Activities. Billy and Susie forfeit participation in sports. They may even get kicked off the team! So what? It was their choice, not yours!

Their Transportation. Take away their wheels. Introduce them to a cardiovascular activity—walking! Confiscate their driver's license, bicycle, skateboard, roller blades. Then "retire" their chauffeur—you!

Freedom. Shorten their curfews and lengthen their chores!

Entertainment. Allow them to experience silence. Don't talk to them for a while. Allow no TV, no music, no video games, no computer . . . just the printed page. They'll start reading, out of desperation!

Naming the problem provides a starting point for discussing the child's problem. Blaming the problem salvages his ego, leaving his self-esteem intact. Retraining is the real beginning of the achievement process. Use rewards when kids are making progress toward their objectives, and don't hesitate to dip into your arsenal of consequences when Billy's achievement motor is on idle.

Perseverance, The Missing Link?

Does it seem to you that each generation bequeaths less and less perseverance to its progeny? Because achievement and success have been described as 5 percent inspiration and 95 percent perspiration, we can't ignore this precious resource. Remember also that self-esteem is highest among doers, attempters, and achievers!

"Thinking impaired," "low-perseverance threshold," and "reluctant learner" are all just "kinder, gentler" terms used to describe lazy students. I'm convinced that laziness is a yet-to-be identified strand in kids' DNA. If little Billy has a case of "hyper-lazy DNA," however, it's time for you to give him a push in order to get him to achieve.

Have you noticed that the sweat-of-the-brow ethic is getting less and less press these days? The child's lack of perseverance may be the result of an overzealous "perfect parent," genuinely interested in providing the child with a better life than he had. This is the parent who says, "I don't want my kids to have to work as hard as I did."

Electables and Negotiables

After you have determined the performance ability of your child and established the grade and behavioral expectations, enlist your child as a participant in his achievement process by allowing him to make some choices. Some of these choices could be where and when to study, but never whether to study!

For example, he may be allowed to choose when to study—with approval from parents. He might select 3:30-4:30, 4:30-5:30, or 5:30-6:30. Starting at third grade, an hour of home study is appropriate. Rule of thumb suggests approximately twenty minutes multiplied by the grade placement—20 (minutes) x 3 (third grade) = 60 minutes. Most high-school students with average ability will spend approximately three hours in daily homestudy.

Avoid late-hour study sessions, if at all possible, except occasionally in order to accommodate a regularly scheduled extracurricular activity. Later in the evening, the child is tired and less likely to complete or produce his best work.

He should be allowed to choose where he studies—his bedroom, living room, dining table, den, etc. Just make sure that his study station is away from frequent interruptions.

Don't underestimate your kids' creativity in excuse-making. Their arsenal of homework excuses equals that of parents' arsenal of consequences. The first rule of parenting is to "stay at least one step ahead of them!"

Absolutely Not-Ables

Once parents have gained some parenting confidence, they have little difficulty establishing the absolutely not-ables that delay the development of responsibility, respect, and the right attitudes in their kids. Here are a few absolutely not-ables that I've used with my own children, recommended at parent workshops, or collected from others. You'll be embellishing this list with some of your own.

1. No electronic entertainment during homestudy sessions, without ability-performance proof—not even on weekends. Applies to TV, stereo, radio, video & computer games.
2. Absence from homestudy sessions is not allowed without parents' permission, and then only as an occasional reward for academic progress.
3. Rudeness and disrespect are not tolerated with family, friends, authority figures, or even small pets.
4. Without exception, be home before curfew or call beforehand with a reason.
5. Chores are not optional. They're partial payment for bed, bath, and board.
6. Purely and simply stated, arguing is not allowed! Parents have to clearly differentiate for kids between time for discussion, and time to *do it.*

Spicing Up Their Gumbo

Some kids don't need spice in their behavior gumbo. If the recipe is perfect, don't mess with it! But there are some who might need just a pinch of salt or their gumbo warmed up a little.

However, Susie's taste buds are begging for spice in her gumbo when she digs her heels in and refuses to follow her parents' rules or her teacher's guidelines for homework assignments. It's time for consequences that get results.

Once you've determined the ability of the child, established appropriate achievement expectations, named and blamed the problem, and set in place the achievement goals, then it's time to expect change.

If observable changes aren't happening, with my clients, I suggest that parents put their child on a contract for action. I've developed a simple Responsibility Contract that involves the use of vegetables as an incentive for improving behavior, attitude, and effort level. Believe me, it's effective! A complete copy of the contract and instructions may be found in appendix F. If you have hesitations about using this action plan, check with your doctor first. He'll probably have a good laugh, then tell you vegetables are good for kids, and remind you that some people survive quite nicely on a steady diet of vegetables throughout their whole life!

Post View and What Parents Can Do

- A child's *capables* should be his *expectables!*

- Kids who are undermotivated do whatever is tolerated by parents.

- If kids are allowed to decide what they do in school, they may decide to do nothing.

- If parents love kids the way they are, they may never see them where they could be.

- Slaying all of a child's dragons weakens her own resourcefulness.

- It's time to call a family meeting when achievement is on less than it should be.

- Your child's teachers spend some thirteen thousand hours with him, first grade through twelfth. Make sure he gets good ones!

- Fuzzy objectives promise minimal effort and blurry achievement.

- Reward the behavior you want repeated.

- An allowance is not an entitlement, so withhold it until you see achievement results.

- Kids respect strength and mock weakness!

- Give your child the "gift of loving limits."

- When kids fail to meet their objectives, hit 'em where it hurts: food, free time, access to friends, allowance, transportation, social calendar, etc.

- Reality discipline includes consequences.

- The most effective achievement plan has a personalized arsenal of consequences.

- Keep copies of the following:
  a. Your child's invitation to the family meeting, and a copy of the agenda,
  b. The objectives for change, and
  c. The specific consequences chosen for objectives not met.

6

Enabling the Learning Disabled

*"Mishaps are like knives,
that either serve us or cut us,
as we grasp them by the blade or the handle."*

—JAMES RUSSELL LOWELL

*C*ontroversy surrounds the issues regarding the identification and treatment of children with special needs. Simply stated, one is likely to find only intermittent consensus among doctors, psychologists, teachers, and parents. I'm not likely to make it to the other end of this chapter without some darts of disagreement from my readers and colleagues.

Disagreement does not shatter my professional feelings, however, because *Raising Achievers* was not written to garner my own professional fan club. I've learned that controversy often gives birth to further study and better solutions. In regard to achievement, that's certainly a worthy goal. The ideas and suggestions presented in this chapter are not capricious, but rather the culmination of years of research and practical experience during my work with hundreds of students and clients. There is no reason why they should not work with your child.

I admit that there will always be exceptions to just about everything—except maybe death and taxes. Just don't allow the exceptions to prevent your child from being one of the successes!

Identifying Learning Disabilities

We've stressed the importance of obtaining an accurate assessment of each child's learning potential. This information could not be more pertinent than it is here as we look at the effects that "labeling" can have for children who have learning "challenges."

Misused labels can *disable,* so I urge you to be very cautious about archiving the wrong information regarding your child's learning ability without professional verification. A valid ability assessment enables you to set realistic expectations with confidence and proceed with appropriate treatment.

In this chapter, we'll be directing our attention to some of the more common mild or even "invisible" disabilities that may be preventing your child from reaching his academic potential. We'll discover what's real and what's hype with regard to each problem. Finally, we'll look at some ways that parents can support the child's classroom instruction with at-home assistance that will expedite and enhance his learning.

Disorders of children are not necessarily disorders of parenting, although sometimes parents are unwarily guilty of contributing to the problem. Reaching one's potential is ultimately the challenge and responsibility of each individual. Parents, teachers, and mentors are merely facilitators!

For example, I'm sure you've probably read or heard about people who've made notable contributions in spite of a learning problem: Nelson Rockefeller, U.S. Vice President, severely dyslexic; Thomas Edison, inventor, self-described as stupid; Woodrow Wilson, U. S. President, non-reader until age eleven; August Rodin,

French sculptor, worst pupil in his class; and Albert Einstein, mathematical genius, language disabled and poor facility for math when young! All these men successfully overcame their initial challenges.

---

*Reaching one's potential is
ultimately the challenge and
responsibility of each individual.*

For discussion, treatment, and services for the more visible learning disabilities—the severely handicapped, physically disabled, or "medically fragile" students—we'll defer to the medical professionals. This is not meant in any way to deny the existence, severity, or needs of these categories of disabilities. It's just more likely that the needs of these more serious disabilities already are under the direction of medical professionals and/or Special-Education personnel in the schools. Generally speaking, parents of these very special children already have some knowledge and information regarding at-home assistance.

Special Education: Background and Issues

Some of you may be unfamiliar with Special Education, especially if your child has never been in the program. Therefore, a quick overview of information about the program and some of its basic guidelines and services is provided here.

Public Laws 94-142 and 99-457 set Special Education guidelines for equivalent educational opportunities for children with learning disorders, to be provided within the "least-restrictive environment." The intent of the law is to help prepare students to integrate into regular society through experiences with students without handicaps. The term, "mainstreaming" stems from this concept of the least-restrictive environment. Mainstreaming, for example, usually means the child is given assistance by a teacher with specialized training in his specific learning disorder, for a period of time during the school day. He is then mainstreamed back into his regular classroom.

Estimates of those with learning disabilities within the school-age population run from 5 to 20 percent. Even if we accept the lower 5 percent figure, the number afflicted with learning disorders is higher than the total of those with mental retardation, cerebral palsy, and epilepsy!

This wide discrepancy in numbers of those affected by learning disorders is due in part to the lack of a specific definition of what constitutes a learning disability. Since 1962, probably a dozen "professional" attempts have evolved in trying to define who comprises the learning-disordered population.

As teachers' responsibilities increase, it is obvious that parents will need to become even more involved with their child's education.

The latest Special Education guidelines expand the concept of least-restrictive environment to "full inclusion." This concept requires regular classroom teachers with little training to monitor students with all types of special needs, such as those with behavior problems that create havoc in the classroom, those who are developmentally delayed, and those with catheters and feeding tubes. Some teachers even have been asked to honor "do not resuscitate" orders if children suffer cardiac arrest in their classrooms.

As teachers' responsibilities increase, it is obvious that parents will need to become even more involved with their child's education, particularly parents of the learning-disabled child.

The initial reaction to full inclusion from teacher groups has not been enthusiastic. Their concern is that their role is changing from one of instructor, for which they have been trained, to one of "care-giver," for which they've not been trained. In a 1994 survey of four hundred teachers, 42 percent opposed full inclusion. Teachers expressed general support for mainstreaming many children with disabilities, saying such moves enable nonhandicapped students to become more sensitive to others' needs while boosting the self-esteem of children who have special challenges. While Special Education is a good idea for some, especially for the more visible, severe handicaps, it may not be the preferred option for others. Parents of children with mild neurological dysfunctions may not want their children labeled "disabled." If these parents are capable, able, and choose to help their own child, then Special Education placement may not be necessary or even desirable.

As a matter of fact, some of the latest data presents a very good case for teaching the child with "suspect-to-mild" disabilities within the regular classroom. One of the benefits most often mentioned is the modeling of appropriate achievement and behavior by the so-called "normal" students. Peer pressure in the regular classroom can be quite effective in encouraging those with learning lags to pick up the pace a bit.

Another issue with Special Education placement is with teacher-pupil ratio. It's rare when Special Education teachers have less than twelve to fourteen students in a class. Even with an instructional aide, the individualized attention and assistance remains questionably insufficient for rapid progress. Qualified, private assistance always has been preferred over group assistance for the most time-efficient academic recovery, just as those who have serious aspirations in sports or music opt for private instruction over group instruction.

Disabling Labeling

Another problem is the label itself, which we've already said can have a disabling effect, particularly when they are incorrectly assigned. Educators, psychologists, and psychiatrists must accept part of the blame for providing far too many learning-label crutches for kids by portraying every frailty and learning resistance as a disorder. One author used the term, "damage-model mania," to describe the professional practice of treating everything as a "sickness."

Behind this damage-model mania may be that there is no Diagnostic and Statistical Manual for "strengths," and strengths are not billable to insurance providers. I'm not alone in my concern that there appears to be a tendency among health care professionals to resort to vocabularies of pathology. This over-diagnosis becomes billable for insurance reimbursement, but it also provides phantom crutches that diminish effort toward achievement.

This damage-model mindset completely bypasses the child's own resilience, motivation, and perseverance in overcoming his problems. Contrary to much of professional and popular thinking, most kids can and will improve if their self image drives them to improve. As parents, we must give our kids this drive by believing in them, expecting them to learn, and providing them with the right guidance and support.

Comprehensive Disability Categories

The following disability categories are those historically classified as having learning problems: Mentally Retarded, Visually Impaired, Hearing Impaired, Orthopedically Impaired, Speech Impaired, Emotionally Disturbed, Learning Disabled, and Other. Of course, some have a combination of several of these disorders.

Forty-one percent of those in Special Education are between the ages of twelve and seventeen. Five percent are between eighteen and twenty-one. Of all those in Special Education, 72 percent are boys and 28 percent are girls.

Who Are The Learning Disabled?

Of the four million students in Special Education from all categories, a little less than 5 percent are classified Learning Disabled (LD). These students are the focus of this chapter, and here are some basic guidelines that have been used for designating an LD student. Incidentally, these descriptions are most likely to find consensus among educators: (1) a discrepancy between achievement and ability; (2) a presumed dysfunction in the child's learning process; (3) the absence of other primary causes of the discrepancy, such as mental retardation, serious emotional disturbances, sensory (seeing/ hearing) deficits, lack of educational opportunity, and cultural inadequacies.

The collective term, "invisible" disabilities, is often applied to LD students, and their problems compared to toothaches. You can't see them, but they're painful nonetheless. Even though the causes of learning disabilities are often uncertain, the lack of achievement is quite evident.

Specific Characteristics of Learning Disabled

Sometimes it's hard to distinguish between a student with a developmental lag and one who is simply not motivated to achieve. However, most LD students do have a similar profile of the following characteristics: learned helplessness, passive toward learning, low self-image, lack of success experience, inept social skills, attention deficits, hyperactivity, impulsiveness, distractibility.

Designer-Label Acronyms

MBD, ND, OR LD? It often depends on who you're talking to. There are several umbrella terms that are used, and these may need some clarification. For the most part, these terms can be used interchangeably.

Minimal Brain Dysfunction (MBD) really is an outdated term. Its use died probably because teachers felt that any problem that had the word brain in the label connoted permanent damage. Teacher expectations for improvement were subsequently small, and little or no real effort to remediate was made.

Neurological Dysfunction (ND) is a broad term frequently used to describe the child who has "difficulty" in learning, especially if that difficulty involves disorders in one or more of the following areas: perception, attention, language, concept formation, memory, or problem solving.

Learning Disabled (LD) is probably the most common group term used for invisible or mild disabilities such as: dyslexia, dyscalculia, dysgraphia, dysorthographia, cerebral dominance, mixed laterality, attention deficit disorder, and hyperactivity. Assistance for these LD problems is the focus of this chapter.

As earlier stated, all labels can have a disabling effect to some degree, especially when they are picked up by kids and used as permission not to persevere in school. The labeled child often excuses herself for poor effort and thinks she's entitled to an inordinate amount of assistance from parents and teachers.

Therefore, the focus of parents' assistance must always be on the problem, *without the label*. If I can raise your awareness in this one area, your kids will not only be achieving at higher levels, but doing so with less dependency on you! The goal of the remaining information in this chapter is helping you determine what's fact and what's myth about learning disabilities.

Behavioral Characteristics of LD Students

At differing levels, LD students can demonstrate any or all of the following behaviors: erratic, inappropriate behavior; persistent hyperactivity; disorganization; distractibility; persistence, even when wrong. So, once his home-study program is in place, one by one, those characteristics that interrupt his attention and learning should be prioritized as behaviors to stop. And, remember, parents, don't allow the level of your "patience" to out pace the level of his "progress" toward a behavioral or learning objective.

How Can Parents Help?

Virtually any normally, intelligent adult can teach or assist a normal child, and that certainly includes you. That's exactly the way millions of children were taught scores of subjects like reading, writing, spelling, geography, science, even classical Latin and Greek. Until the early 19th century, European masters or scholars in specific trade and/or subject areas taught others quite successfully, and I might add, without benefit of a single teacher-education course!

Parents, remember, you're acting only in a support role. The classroom teacher still provides your child with the bulk of his instruction, including help which accommodates his particular learning disability.

Parents, please note . . . the discussion that follows will focus on specific learning disabilities, and I have used the same terms as those used by special-education teachers. You may wish to skim through the areas that do not hold special interest or that do not relate to your own child's particular needs.

Dyslexia

There are two very divided schools of thought regarding dyslexia. One theory espoused by Dr. Peter Breggin, author of *Toxic Psychiatry*, concludes that dyslexia is not scientifically proven, but rather a parents' movement born of frustration. Psychologist Dr. Rosemond agrees and treats dyslexia as a theoretical disorder with characteristics that reflect the lack of left-right directionality maturation.

Those taking the opposing view define Dyslexia as a neurological dysfunction resulting in mild to severe difficulty in learning to read and understanding the meaning of words. Dyslexia often is accompanied by comprehension problems as well.

Several Characteristics Associated with Dyslexia

1. Persistent difficulty with perception, discrimination, and memory of printed symbols, letters, words.
2. Persistent confusion or reversal of letters or words: tub/but, saw/was, felt/left.
3. Persistent difficulty in grasping the meaning of words or remembering what is read.
4. Some reports of actual movement of letters and words on the page during reading.

What's Hype, What's Real About Dyslexia?

Dyslexia is said to affect up to 15 percent of the population, and contrary to popular belief, it affects boys and girls fairly equally, so say three separate studies. But then there are also several other large studies reporting the opposite, finding the ratio of boys to girls with reading impairments to be 4 to 1.

Some think this discrepancy between ratios of boys and girls with reading disabilities has to do with the differences in behavior of boys and girls. Girls tend not to draw the level of attention to themselves as do boys with their more aggressive behavior. It's argued that teachers may tend to "notice" and subsequently identify reading problems of boys more than those of girls who may struggle more quietly.

However, in some recent research, neuroscientists are reporting some neurobiological bases of dyslexia which have been suspected for almost a century. Anomalies in the biological structure of dyslexic brains show some brain asymmetry that deviates from the norm. A genetic basis for dyslexia is also indicated by studies of families and twins that find strong evidence of a tendency to inherit dyslexia. These studies are still inconclusive, however, at this time. A child who is merely slow learning to read is not dyslexic! Dyslexia is probably one of the most misapplied LD labels. A little knowledge about dyslexia often can be a dangerous thing. I've known many teachers and parents who've either given or accepted this label without conducting sufficient tests to rule out other factors that could be causing the delay in learning to read.

As a reading clinician for many years myself, I have developed these theories about dyslexia.

1. Occasional letter reversals up through age eight are not abnormal.
2. Few adults exhibit reversals, and it is therefore considered a maturational problem.
3. If letter-number reversals occur because the child sees things backwards, it would follow that these backward behaviors would be observed in other spatial/directional activities like reaching for the fork or the glass of water on the wrong side of the plate.

Real or hype, both sides agree that children with dyslexic characteristics can be taught to read when their specific difficulties are accurately identified. However, other related problems like the following should be ruled out before assigning a dyslexia label: latent laterality (left-right development), phonic deficits, poor study skills, vocabulary meaning, vision problems, poor effort, and hearing deficits.

How Are Dyslexic Tendencies Improved?

1. Make sure your child masters his phonic sounds, and for fourth grade and up, also the syllabication rules. See section on reading in chapter 9.
2. Listen to your child read at least three pages daily from an age/grade-appropriate book.
3. Establish a three-word-error maximum per page as his word accuracy goal.
4. Have him tell you what the word means if there is a hint that he doesn't know.
5. Have him make vocabulary cards for the words he doesn't know, with the new word on one side and a very brief definition on the other side. Understanding words is what comprehension is all about, so stress the importance of learning new words.
6. While watching TV, during commercial breaks, after reading a book or a story, ask the following "journalistic" questions: Who, What, When, Where, Why, How? Who are the main characters? Where does the story take place? What's the problem? What steps have been taken to solve the problem? What do you think they'll do next? How would you have done it differently? What else would you like to know about this? These are all comprehension questions that exercise the child's basic comprehension skills, like gathering knowledge, sequencing events, predicting outcomes, making judgments, forming opinions, drawing conclusions, etc. By merely changing the vocabulary level of the questioning, this exercise is appropriate for all ages.

Dyscalculia

Dyscalculia is defined as difficulty understanding math concepts, mastery of math facts, and abstract math-system reasoning. There is less information available on dyscalculia than there is on dyslexia, although there are some who report a correlation between the two. In my own practice, I've had many clients with reading impairments who did very well in math.

Several Characteristics of Dyscalculia
1. Difficulty understanding math concepts, including math vocabulary.
2. Difficulty memorizing math facts.
3. Difficulty remembering math facts once learned.
4. Extreme difficulty with math word problems.
5. Difficulty remembering steps in solving math problems.
6. Difficulty remembering math concepts from one test to the next.

What's Real, What's Hype About Dyscalculia?

Persistence and intensity of these six behaviors, even after directed attention to them, usually indicate that a real problem exists. However, the failure to set short-term goals for learning the necessary math-system steps and concepts, or failure to levy appropriate incentives should not cause a child to be labeled as dyscalculic.

How is Dyscalculia Improved?
1. Work very closely with your child's teacher, requesting additional worksheets on every concept with which he's having difficulty.
2. Reward every major math hurdle he masters: addition facts, subtraction facts, multiplication facts, division facts, measurement, telling time, fraction-percentage equivalents, etc.
3. See that he turns in all math homework. Highlight errors, provide occasional reteaching in problem areas, and recheck his corrected work.
4. Involve him in all of the age-appropriate, math-related, real-world uses of math: paying bills, making the family budget, reconciling bank statements; figuring interest, making change, figuring mileage and distance; measuring for cooking; computing areas for painting, wallpapering, carpeting, woodcrafting, etc.

There is a high correlation between relevance and learning. When learning is made practical to a child, there is less resistance to mastery. One author said that he had his children, by age twelve, start writing out the checks for paying the family bills. Of course, he signed the checks. Having them write the checks gave them practical knowledge of household expenditures and probably helped them to understand why they were asked to turn off lights!

Dysgraphia

Dysgraphia varies from having difficulty writing to the almost complete inability to write. This problem can be the result of perceptual and/or neurological disorders or actual damage to the nerves controlling muscles in the arm and hand. If teachers indicate that the problem appears serious, parents may be advised to see a neurologist to rule out a false assumption.

Several Characteristics of Dysgraphia
1. Distortions of letters or numbers.
2. Very large or very small letters or numbers.
3. Erratic or cramped spacing between words.
4. Inappropriate alignment of numbers in math.
5. Inability to "predict" space and/or adhere to margins.
6. Laborious, slow writing of letters or numbers.
7. Stressed out by pencil/paper assignments.
8. Overall messy or illegible written work.

What's Hype, Wxhat's Real About Dysgraphia?
I did clinical teaching for nine years, and my students were very reluctant learners. My task was to ignite their interest in learning. Believe me, I've seen my share of "hieroglyphic" handwriting! My sense is that most of my students simply weren't interested or motivated enough to want to improve. These students had a history of no homework, no effort, no interest, and no parental push.

Without some background information or medical history on kids with this profile, it's a judgment call as to which came first, the chicken or the egg. Was their handwriting poor because they simply lacked sufficient writing exercise to perfect the skill? Or did they develop a distaste for writing and doing their homework because writing was slow and laborious?

In all my years in the field, I've seen only a handful of students I'd classify as dysgraphic. But I also admit that I'm not always able to fully evaluate outside factors that influence the development of good handwriting skills, such as parent and teacher expectations, handwriting objectives, and appropriate use of rewards and consequences.

Sometimes teachers contribute to the problem by allowing work to be done in printing rather than cursive handwriting. Printing is slower, and as assignments increase in length, cursive handwriting allows the student to complete her homework more quickly.

I remember one suspected dysgraphic client, a model student in every sense of the word, enthusiastic, persevering, bright. He also had very interested, supportive parents. In fact, he had been home schooled up to seventh grade, which was a clue to his labored handwriting. He'd never been required to do handwriting, and his was at about beginning-third-grade speed. He knew how to do cursive, but he lacked four years of practice. I recommended an evaluation by a neurologist, but the doctor found no neural pathology.

How Is Dysgraphia Improved?

Here are some basic suggestions for developing and improving handwriting after parents have set expectations and selected the appropriate consequences as needed.

1. An appropriate place to write with good lighting, a smooth surface, and sufficient space.
2. Good writing tools: #2 pencils, erasers, sharpener, erasable ballpoint pens, and plenty of paper.
3. Basic printing and cursive examples of correct letter and number formation.
4. Pencil-grip instruction and pencil-grip trainers if child does not have a three-finger pencil grip. This is important to prevent muscle cramps in the hand and arm as the length of assignments increases.

5. Proper placement of paper. The forearm of the hand used for writing and the vertical plane of the paper should have approximately the same slant.
6. The head's proximity to the paper should be the distance of the chin resting in the palm to the elbow on the writing surface.
7. Follow these handwriting suggestions: Use the width of thumb knuckle for paragraph indentations. Use an index finger as the space between words. Cross all the appropriate letters. Keep all printing or cursive writing on the lines of the paper. Use proper upper and lower case. Adhere to right and left margins of the paper.

One last word about handwriting from a teacher's perspective. With the advent of computers, there is some legitimacy to the argument that handwriting is not as important as it once was. But, until we've reached the point that each student has a computer and printer at home, in the classroom, and maybe in his pocket, good handwriting skills are necessary. One upper elementary teacher estimates that she "deciphers" approximately thirty thousand papers each year! Have mercy on teachers' eyes and see that your Billy and Susie turn in neat, legible homework. When they bring messy homework in for your signature, say, "Not bad for a first draft. Do your best recopying, and I'm sure your next draft will be ready for my signature."

Dysorthographia

Dysorthographia is difficulty with the mechanics of spelling. It is thought that as with dysgraphia, its origins are neurobiologic in nature. Problems with the brain's processing of visual, perceptual, and auditory stimuli contribute to this disorder.

Characteristics and What's Real or Hype?

The child who really has demonstrated spelling accuracy mid-week on a pretest and fails the Friday spelling test could have dysorthographia. However, it is difficult to determine what part of his problem is related to mnemonics (memory techniques) and what part is neurobiologic in origin.

Inability or great difficulty in achieving consistent accuracy in spelling a prescribed list of words, even after instruction in memory techniques, is even stronger evidence of possible dysorthographia.

Continual reversal or omission of letters could indicate a mix of dyslexic and dysgraphic tendencies, especially if the test is written. If the child is able to correctly spell the words orally but unable to spell the same words on a written test, then the child may have a predominantly auditory preference for processing and learning. In other words, he may be an auditory learner rather than a visual learner. The child who spells in a way that barely resembles the words from his spelling list could be having difficulty hearing rhythms and syllables. He also may not know the simple rules for breaking words into syllables. (See Appendix B, Read Right Away, Card #16 for the syllabication rules.) Missing one or two spelling words on weekly tests does not indicate dysorthographia.

What Can Be Done to Improve Dysorthographia?
1. Study spelling words for approximately fifteen minutes. Look carefully and pronounce each word.
2. Note double and/or silent letters by highlighting.
3. Divide each word into syllables.
4. Pronounce each word by syllables.
5. As words are dictated, spell the words, one syllable at a time, orally.
6. Highlight only the "missed parts" of words during oral spelling. Study these words again.
7. Write spelling words from dictation.
8. Review and correct by highlighting spelling errors.
9. Review spelling words the night before the spelling test.
10. Give a surprise reward at the end of the month for perfect weekly spelling tests.

Attention-Deficit Hyperactivity Disorder

In 1990, the news media carried the story of the discovery of the first specific abnormality in the brains of people with hyperactivity.

In 1993, a genetic cause was added. Researchers found that hyperactivity is especially common among people with a condition known as thyroid-hormone resistance, which runs in families.

Technically, hyperactivity is known as Attention Deficit Hyperactivity Disorder, ADHD. It's the most common psychiatric disorder of childhood and is said to effect between 2 and 4 percent of school-age children. About half the time, some aspects of the disorder persist into adulthood. Hyperactivity often runs in families. In one study of twenty-five adults, hyperactive since childhood, each reported they were now parents of hyperactive children.

Children can have ADD without the "Hyperactive" component associated with those diagnosed as ADHD.

Several Characteristics of ADD and ADHD

The ADD/ADHD child cannot be distinguished from the normal child on the playground. He doesn't run faster or play harder. It's just that he can't shift down to low gear when it's appropriate for him to do so. One child described his own problem as having all channels of a TV set coming into his brain at the same time, without having a channel tuner. Mothers report restless, active infants becoming children who stand and walk at early ages, then proceed to destroy the house!

The ADD child may be the "dreamer" or the "space cadet" who has difficulty staying focused on an assigned task, while the ADHD child is the one more likely to get the attention of his teachers and parents. Researchers, doctors, teachers, and parents list the following common attributes:

1. Inattentive, impulsive, and incessantly in motion.
2. Tends to blurt out answers without thinking.
3. Runs into the street without looking.
4. Constantly fidgets, squirms, and jumps about.
5. Troubles parents and teachers with a hot temper and frequent disobedience.
6. Over-talkative as well as overactive.
7. Unable to sustain interest for long periods.

8. Academic underachiever.
9. Low self-esteem.

What's "Real" About ADHD?

The research that found this metabolic abnormality in ADHD subjects was reported in the *New England Journal of Medicine*. Brain scans of adults afflicted with the disorder since childhood showed that their brain cells were "8 percent less active" than those of normal people. This reduced activity was especially dramatic in the parts of the brain that control attention and inhibit behavior. In another study, brain activity in ADHD adults was significantly reduced in 30 of 60 specific regions of the brain.

What's "Hype" About ADHD?

All that's hyperactive is not hyperactivity. Some of it's hype! There is probably no other learning disability that is the subject of so much controversy as ADHD. The reason is that without the benefit of a brain scan, ADHD cannot be truly quantified or verified. ADHD is being called the "designer label" disorder because only the wealthy can afford proof of its existence. Most ADHD experts in the medical field admit that without these very expensive tests, ADHD diagnosis relies on the degree and history of its characteristics as demonstrated earlier.

Some educators take the posture that kids must learn to pay attention now, or pay later. As an example, read one teacher's observations on John:

> not sitting still; hitting kids; talking out loud; interrupts; not doing his work; line breaker; stretching boundaries; few friends, mostly older; peers want to kill him; can't get his letters; can't use scissors; couldn't share; couldn't take turns.

Permit me to add a few comments about ADHD based upon my own training, fairly extensive research on the subject, and experience with thousands of kids.

- In reference to that 8 percent reduced brain-cell activity in ADHD subjects, why not focus on finding ways to help kids learn to initiate their attention and behavior controls that will allow the other 92 percent of the brains to function at the maximum level?
- If other methods prove ineffective after ardent effort, medication such as Ritalin, Cylert, or Dexedrine may be a viable alternative. The child's education is at stake here.
- In reference to the ADHD characteristics given earlier, I believe many of those characteristics can be more correctly assessed and identified as the result of ineffective discipline and/or "kid" problems, rather than learning disorders.
- Whether or not ADHD is real, it is not the only critical issue in underachievement. ADHD seems to get an inordinate amount of attention from the media and professionals. There are many other significant factors that equally impact learning, such as intelligence, attitude, behavior, and responsibility.

How Is ADHD Improved?

In any case, since they're not doing brain transplants as of the writing of this book, and the benefits of psychostimulant drugs are both controversial and imperfect, the more prudent choice might be to concentrate on maximizing the brains your child has. So whether you have a child with brain-scan-identified ADHD, or a history of an intense degree of ADHD characteristics, here are some suggestions that may focus his attention and help him to control his behavior:

1. Clearly-defined rules, expectations, and instructions.
2. Firm, predictable, and swift consequences.
3. A team approach by parents and the classroom teacher.
4. In extreme cases or when otherwise warranted, doctor-monitored use of stimulant drugs—Ritalin, Cylert, or Dexedrine—to assist in behavior control and concentration.

Here are some additional non-drug techniques for ADHD that parents can try. Simply give the classroom teacher permission to use some of the following to determine if there are any beneficial effects on behavior, attention, and academic productivity:

1. The child wears a rubber band on his wrist and pops himself when he's becoming inattentive or acting inappropriately. His teacher provides the cue that it's "pop" time.
2. The child wears a surgical mask over her mouth as a reminder to modify excessive talking at inappropriate times.
3. The child inserts ear plugs when classroom cacophony is affecting his attention, but not during lectures.
4. The child goes behind a "study screen" to help her stay on task.
5. The child buckles his safety-release "desk belt" as a reminder to stay seated when appropriate.
6. The child rechannels excessive energy by doing push-ups or jumping jacks, jumping rope, or running.
7. In order to discourage peer interaction, teacher assigns appropriate classroom seating, not time out, which is minimally effective for ADHD kids.

For relaxation and calming, the parent may wish to explore the benefits of using a massager or soft vegetable brush on the child. Using downward strokes, start at the base of his skull and proceed to the tips of his toes while he lies on his stomach. This can be done before leaving for school and prior to beginning homework. There are also vibrator chairs available that provide similar relaxation stimulation.

Cerebral Dominance (CD) and Mixed Laterality (ML)

Some early researchers into reading problems suggested that lack of cerebral dominance in the left hemisphere of the brain, the language area, could contribute to certain neurobiologic learning disabilities, particularly reading-related disorders. The tendencies to reverse letters and words are given as common characteristics of this disorder.

Current findings suggest that even though the left hemisphere controls language functions and the right hemisphere controls the nonverbal functions, both hemispheres contribute to the learning process. Faulty "firing or wiring" in either hemisphere reduces learning efficiency, acquisition, and use of language. Scientific research in this area is quite controversial, and the results are inconclusive.

Mixed Laterality (ML) is the term used to describe a related problem, which is also controversial because of mixed results. *Established laterality* is the preference for performing all functions on one side of the body—hand, eye, and foot. *Mixed laterality* is the tendency to mix the right and left preference in using hands, eyes, and feet. Educators, including myself, report learning problems more often with mixed laterality when eye preference (rather than foot preference) is opposite to that of the hand. I direct my attention to *eye* preference, and it's really quite simple to determine your child's eye preference. Follow these steps.

1. Have your child stand about ten feet away, facing you.
2. Have him hold a tube (made from rolled-up paper or empty paper towel spool) in his preferred hand, with arm stretched out stiff in front of him.
3. Have him look through the tube at your nose, while he keeps both of his eyes open.
4. Determine his eye preference by identifying which eye you see looking through the tube at your nose.

From my private clients and those requesting testing through some five hundred schools over the last ten years, approximately 75 percent have ML. Educational literature projects approximately 38 percent of a random population to be ML. The reason I find a much higher incidence of ML in my testing is that I am assessing students who've been referred because they are already exhibiting characteristics of those with learning problems.

My experience is that ML does effect learning in many students, particularly in reading. Such a high percentage of these ML students being referred by parents or teachers for our testing and/or private assistance programs defies other explanation.

I've also found that those who have a right-hand preference and left-eye (RH/LE) preference are most likely to experience reading-related learning difficulties. Let me explain how and why this happens.

First let's assume that these RH/LE children have established left-brain cerebral dominance for language processing, because scientific research indicates (by extrapolation) that 90 percent of all right-handers are left-brain cerebral dominant, and reading is a left-brain activity. All visual stimuli enter the left hemisphere as upside-down images, then travel across the midbrain to the right hemisphere to turn the visual image right side up. Finally, the image then must travel back across the midbrain to the left hemisphere for language-based processing or decoding. It's theorized that some neural misfiring, misfiled data, or frustration occurs during this extra trip across trillions of neurons!

Those with right-hand preference and right-eye (RH/RE) preference and a left-hemisphere cerebral dominance bypass this last step. Visual stimuli come into the right hemisphere, then cross the midbrain to the left hemisphere as the final step to both reverse the upside-down image and to begin processing the visual information received.

I admit that this is a very crude explanation for such a highly technical subject. It certainly does not pretend to cover all of the controversial areas, such as right-brain CD, mixed-brain CD, other preexisting, related learning handicaps, brain trauma, varying degrees of intelligence, and effort levels.

There is exciting new brain research through imaging technology such as PET, CT, MRI, and BEAM that allows brain activity to be traced and mapped during the performance of various functions. Costs for these sophisticated tests preclude common use, but as researchers continue to study the brain, new insights are promised regarding neurobiological bases of learning disabilities and disorders.

What's Real, What's Hype About CD and ML?

According to doctors there is only one generally agreed upon method for establishing CD, and that is the Wada Method, which involves injection of a barbiturate to anesthetize one hemisphere of the brain at a time and conduct language-based tests. Since these tests cannot be conducted by general clinicians, classroom teachers, or psychologists, data for determining CD is through generalizations from Wada-type studies. These data report that 90 percent of right-handers and 64 percent of left-handers are left-hemisphere CD.

What Can Be Done to Help Those with ML?

Genetic, observational, and medical data seem to indicate that each of us is born with our cerebral dominance and laterality already established. Some research of the learning-disabled population, without other specific brain damage, finds no more ML, left-handers, or right-handers than are found in the general population. (I would question the validity of their diagnostics used to determine ML.)

Still other research shows that lack of laterality is often accompanied by left-right confusion and a high incidence of problems in reading, comprehension, handwriting, and coordination.

Finally, many educational therapists and neurologists report finding that students are more likely to experience academic success with less stress when hand, eye, and foot preference are on one side.

Therefore, here are some suggestions for encouraging hand-eye "unilaterality" (same-side dominance), which may assist your child in processing information received visually. The following suggested activities are to be used approximately one and one-half hours a day for approximately four months. They are suggested only for those mixed laterally and also having difficulty in reading or math. If your child has no problems in reading or math, then we assume ML is not a problem.

1. Place a red filter over the preferred eye.
2. Do written homework assignments using erasable red pen or pencil with the preferred eye red-filtered.

3. Cover the TV screen with a red plastic filter and view TV while wearing a red eye filter.
4. Play jacks with a red filter over the eye, using red jacks and a red ball. This is an excellent hand-eye coordination activity for all ages!
5. Play table tennis using a reddish-orange ping-pong ball, while wearing the red filter.

The purpose of the red filter is to prevent the eye that is filtered from seeing what is written in red. This forces the brain to process what is written in red by the opposite eye—the one in "lateral training."

Red-filter glasses are inexpensive and may be purchased from local Optometric Associations. Or, you can make your own, as well as a red filter for your TV screen, from a red plastic book report cover available in most stationery stores.

1. From one edge of the red plastic book report cover, cut a piece to fit in the frame of a pair of cheap sunglasses. Cover the dominant eye and leave the other eye unfiltered.
2. Use the remaining uncut piece of plastic as a TV screen filter. This can be attached at the top of the screen with a small piece of masking tape and flipped out of the way for non-training viewing.
3. If your child wears glasses, purchase red cellophane from a florist or craft shop and place it over the lens of his dominant eye.

Have your child spend one and one-half hours daily for approximately four months using the red-filter activities listed. Much of this time can be spent doing homework. The remaining dominance-training time could be spent in far-point activities (TV watching, ping pong, jacks, etc.). He can get his training time within the classroom if he prefers. However, the training is more easily monitored when it is done at home. The embarrassment factor from peer teasing is also eliminated when the training occurs at home.

This is a vision-safe activity, because during the red-filter sessions, only the color red is restricted from the eye wearing the red filter. The unfiltered eye "in training" sees red. However, check with your eye-care professional if you have any concerns prior to using these activities.

Post View and What Parents Can Do

- Seek professional assessment for problems suspected to be serious, especially if your child's teacher is urging this.

- Set short-term objectives for progress in specific areas of need.

- Use rewards and consequences as appropriate.

- Focus on the child's strengths, rather than weaknesses, in setting expectations.

- Substitute objectives and goals for labels.

- Check all homework before it is turned in, for neatness, accuracy, and following directions.

- Be sure your patience level doesn't exceed your child's progress level.

- Communicate frequently with your child's teacher, and support him or her in every way.

- Take self-addressed, postage-paid envelopes for your child's teacher to use for notes to you.

- Visit your child's class to observe his behavior, his special presentations,etc.

7

Homework without the (Parents') Hassle

"Something has got to be done about
homework in this country.
Parents just can't handle it anymore."

—ERMA BOMBECK

*A*ccording to Erma Bombeck, "The energy it takes to raise a child is comparable to climbing the Pyramids in heels every day carrying a bucket of ice to the top before it melts." Well, if you thought night feedings, colic, and potty training were bad, just wait until you're faced with years of nightly homework hassles . . . with each and every one of your children! That's reality, unless you're ready to follow a few "hassle-free" (well, okay, "less"-hassle) homework guidelines.

This chapter is about how you can help your child develop responsibility, reach his potential, and realize his unique excellence.

Excellence is doing something better than most. Maybe the whole purpose of individuality is this excellence. The child who earns A's on his report card, designs his own science project, participates in a piano recital or school play, campaigns for student body president, or creates a piece of art is expressing his own uniqueness and individuality. One of the greatest gifts a parent can give a child is the gift of encouragement toward excellence! Isn't excellence the real essence of homework? Isn't daily homework really a microcosm of overall achievement? It's been said that work can do more to advance a child than his parents' wealth. The question parents have to ask themselves is, "Am I ready to make this commitment?"

I'll be challenging you in this chapter not to allow yourself to be swayed by your child's cries of, "This is too hard." Thomas Edison said, "Opportunity is missed by most people because it is dressed in overalls and looks like work." Want proof? Look at just a few of the following statistics regarding homework.

Two-thirds of high-school students do less than one hour of homework. Catholic schools have the highest academic scores, probably because they also give and get more homework from kids! In state-wide testing, eighth graders showed an 84 point increase on a 400 point scale with two hours of homework. With one hour of homework, the increase was only 19 points. Seniors showed a 63 point increase on the same 400 point scale with two hours of homework compared with only a 34 point increase with only one hour of homework.

The more time we spend doing something, the better we get at it, whether it's sports, music, art, or learning. Practice produces excellence. As a former state school superintendent commented, "Too long, we've been leaning on the shovels of low expectations."

Some of our brightest students are getting what one writer called a "dumbed-down" education because of resistance to homework. Learning is like building with blocks. Teachers can only add to the building as each preceding block is stable and in place. When kids are reluctant and careless about doing homework, they fail to master the concept and skill prerequisites for subsequent instruction. The student's lack of concept mastery ultimately limits the teacher's effectiveness.

The quality of education in America is everyone's responsibility, not just educators. Teachers have no real controls when it comes to the student's responsibility for achievement. Grades are teachers' only clout; and passive learners couldn't care less about grades, unless parents make them care.

"Opportunity is missed by most people because it is dressed in overalls and looks like work."
—Thomas Edison

We're finding that kids today lack drive and imagination, as well as the ability to analyze, critique, and think through problems. One comedian referred to this malady as being "logically impaired." Brain experts say there's proof that we must "use it or lose it." So the more we stretch our minds, the better and longer they will serve us. Researchers have found that biochemical changes occur in mentally-engaged minds. These changes allow more effective and cognitive functioning, particularly in areas of attention and memory. One researcher reported that the intellectually active mind increases brain cell health and size, and that mentally-engaged people are generally happier and better adjusted.

The Need for Responsibility

Do you know why kids don't form support groups for their anxieties? They don't need to; they already have two very supportive adult allies to dump all their anxieties on—Mom and Dad! For example, Dr. Kevin Leman tells the story of a mom who received a frantic telephone call from her son that went something like this:

Son: Mom, you've gotta hurry home, cause we've got this big test tomorrow!

123

Mom: I'm sorry, son. You have this big test tomorrow. I have a tennis lesson.

In the article, "In Praise of the 'F' Word" Newsweek, May 1991, author Mary Sherry, tells the story about her son who preferred talking to his friends in the back of the class rather than "wasting" any of his intellectual talents in his senior English class. In a conference with his teacher, Mary queried why the teacher hadn't moved her son to the front of the class, believing the embarrassment would settle him down. His English teacher's reply was, "I don't move seniors. I *flunk* them." Guess what? When Mary relayed this message to her son, he got down to business and finished the semester with an A!

You've heard the saying, "Give a man a fish, and you feed him for a day. Teach him to fish, and you feed him for life." Likewise, help a child do his homework, and he may get an A on his homework. Teach him to how to do his own homework, and you develop an independent learner for life (and relieve yourself of the nightly hassle)! You can begin now, by setting some ground rules for homework.

Homework Ground Rules

1. Homework comes first. Set daily, home study sessions at the same time, Monday through Friday. No discussion, no complaints, no exceptions, case closed.
2. See that your child's study area is stocked with all the age/grade appropriate study stuff.
3. A parent is to be available as a homework manager during the established home study session. It is appropriate to provide a few minutes of brief explanation or to review the child's homework progress. However, this assistance is made available only at fifteen to twenty minute intervals. When the study session time is over, the parent-homework-manager is off duty!
4. Upon completion of homework, the child is to report to the parent that homework is completed, present the

homework (as proof) for parent signature, be excused from home study, and place homework in a school-work basket on a table by the front door.

5. The parent *does not* play detective with questions of, "Have you finished your homework? Are you sure? Where is it?"

6. It is suggested that the parents issue the child his evening meal ticket in exchange for his completed homework. No homework, no meal ticket. (Remember, "If a man doesn't work, he doesn't eat.") This should cure homework delays of "In a minute," and "When I get around to it."

Rewards of Responsibility

Responsibility has its rewards as illustrated by the story about the high-school senior whose responsibility and grade quickly turned around after his English teacher threatened to flunk him. This is true for high-school seniors interested in graduation and grade-point averages for college entrance, as well as for most all enthusiastic learners and scholars. Unfortunately, grades alone are not nearly as important to the elementary child, and even less important to passive learners and LD children, unless parents carefully establish the importance of grades from the start.

What do grades mean anyway? The answer is, a lot. Even though each teacher's grades may come from a slightly different reference point, there is little argument that an A represents excellence, and that Ds and Fs are definitely below-effort counterparts. As and Bs are grades earned by bright students with the right attitude and reasonable effort. Cs are usually for average students, but are also given to bright students who apply very little effort. From most teachers' perspectives, Ds and Fs are unacceptable-effort grades, or possibly grades earned by students who may be misplaced in the tracking system.

Report cards also show the child's strengths that the teacher has observed. Some strengths will be in non-academic areas—music, art, P.E., cooperation, sharing, politeness. All kids have some strengths. Recognize and compliment him for his strengths, and you validate him as a worthwhile individual. The child with a history of underachievement especially needs this self-esteem boost. Recognition and complimenting provide incentive and achievement payoffs.

Wise parents will select a variety of rewards for the improving student—small ones, big ones, surprise ones, fun ones, and most important, motivating ones. These might include expanded freedom, extended curfews, extra privileges, increased allowances, video rentals, camping trips, special desserts, no chores for a week, dining out, going on a picnic, a new CD, etc. These are just a few examples well worth the time, planning, and money. What's the price of an excited learner? What's it worth to you to be relieved of the homework hassle?

Responsibility Requires Practice

Study is an arduous task, "a weariness of the flesh," according to Solomon (Eccl. 12;12, KJV). Whew! Am I relieved! I was afraid I wasn't normal. I think most writers would agree with me that one of the loneliest experiences is that of staring at the blank computer screen with its impatient, blinking cursor beckoning for words of lucidity and brilliance.

Any number of examples could be cited that are the result of practice to perfect one's performance: juggling, acrobatics, gymnastics, martial arts, race-car driving, running, skating, Olympic sports, theater arts, opera, music, art, science. The list is almost infinite.

But here's just one reminder of the rewards of practice that you can share with your child: The brilliant and prolific Thomas Edison had some one thousand failures before he succeeded in perfecting his light bulb!

Responsibility Requires Self-Discipline

Responsibility requires perseverance, a key element of self discipline. Draw your child's attention to the second part of the compound word, homeWORK. In my experience, most of my classroom students and my private clients really expected to get an A for their first draft of an essay, book report, or research paper. No, what they'd really prefer is that parents did it for them. But, remember, our focus in this chapter is getting kids self-disciplined and responsible for doing their own homework and promoting parents to positions of homework managers.

Parents As Homework Managers

Longfellow said, "Discipline is like a bridled horse with the reins held lightly." Parents, resist the tendency to give inflated praise and to accept less than your child's best ability-based effort in his homework. We've already stressed the importance of knowing what her ability is. So stop wondering whether or not her brain has a left hemisphere. Through testing, you've checked, and she does! So when her enthusiasm for learning shows the energy level of a slug, are you going to keep singing to her, "I've got high hopes, high-in-the-sky, apple-pie hopes"? Definitely not!

You're going to state confidently, in a straight-forward, clear manner, using your unmistakable voice of authority, "Billy/Susie, these are the grades your mother (father) and I expect to see on your next report card." Then state the grades that are realistic and reachable for your child.

As home study managers, parents are to see that their children consistently turn in quality homework. Parents should do no more and no less than a good work supervisor would do for an employee with an assigned task.

Establishing Subject-Grade Expectations

Perhaps one of the most important assets a child can have is belief in his ability. Challenge your child to project realistic grades for his subjects. As Henry Ford stated, "If you think you can do a thing or think you can't do a thing, you're right." *Belief in our ability*, makes us stay at it until we prove that we can!

According to Thomas Mann, "Order and simplification are the first steps toward the mastery of a subject . . . the actual enemy is the unknown." When I read this quote, I thought about the notebooks of underachievers that we spoke of earlier. Your child's notebook is equally, if not more, important to his achievement than his textbooks, because his notebook holds all his assignments, class notes, corrected tests, and study guides. I've also seen students open their notebooks to the middle of a clean-paper section and begin doing their homework. Later they're unable to locate the homework they actually did complete. This is inefficiency not *about* to happen, but *in process!* So, make sure Billy and Susie have well-organized notebooks, where they can put their finger on any subject, any test, assignment sheet, corrected work and tests, and clean paper instantly.

From Homework to Homestudy

I've now renamed homework to homestudy. The reason I've done this is simple. The next time Billy requests that he be excused from homework today with his "I've already done my homework at school" or "I don't have any homework tonight," try this on him. "That's great, honey. Now you'll have time during your regular homestudy to read your book for your upcoming book report or time to get to the library to do your research for your science project."

When there is no formal homework assignment, or when it was truly completed at school, is an excellent time for Susie to study vocabulary words or spelling words, memorize some "fuzzy" math facts, edit or redraft a report in process, or simply read a good book!

For a student who is well on his way to an A, backed up by evidence such as his most recent report card or progress report, it's okay to recognize his progress and reward him by allowing him to negotiate for a "free-from-homestudy" day! But do exercise caution here, as kids are experts at taking the proverbial "inch" and stretching it to a mile!

The responsibility of confident parents is to impress upon Billy and Susie that roller-blading is not a higher calling than homework. Change this mindset! Little league, volleyball practice, TV, and playing Nintendo with friends are also low-to-zero priorities when their grades are slipping and the homestudy session clock is ticking. Only profuse bleeding from gaping wounds or high fevers are allowed to interrupt the daily homestudy regimen!

Your kids will get serious about their homework when they realize you are. When daily homestudy sessions become as routine as meal time and bath time, homework complaints vanish. I had a mother tell me once that she couldn't get her second grader to do his homework. I asked her if she allowed her young Timmy to refuse to take a bath or brush his teeth.

Parents, allow your kids to learn from experience what Anthony Trollope wrote in his autobiography: "A small daily task, if it be really daily, will beat the labors of a spasmodic Hercules."

For projecting your child's grades for each subject, you might want to use the following sample form and procedure.

GRADE PROJECTION SHEET

Subject	Student Projected Grade	Parent Projected Grade	Teacher Projected Grade	Actual Grade
Reading	C	B	B	
Math	D	B	C+	
Etc.				

1. List each core subject, like reading, math, science, and history, in the first column.
2. In the second column, beside each subject, have your child list the letter grades that he feels will represent his best effort.
3. Review the grades he's listed, and based upon your knowledge of his ability and previous effort in a particular subject, appropriately modify his projected grades and enter your projections in the third column.
4. Have his teacher enter grade projections based upon his ability in the fourth column.

5. Enter the actual grades your child receives on his report card in the fifth column. Keep these as a handy reference of his academic improvement.

It's rather interesting to see whose grade projections match the grades he actually receives. In any case, the grade projections in column three or four should be his target goals.

"A small daily task,
if it be really daily, will beat the
labors of a spasmodic Hercules."
—Anthony Trollope

One important and final step in projecting grades is to have your child verbalize his grade expectations to others—parents, teachers, and friends. This step is verbal validation that he believes he can reach his goal. He's also more likely to increase his effort because he doesn't want to lose face.

Conclusion

If you want to "de-stress" the hassles with your child's homework, follow the guidelines presented here. Stop with the *helping* and go with the *managing* side of homework. Managers delegate responsibility. Delegate kids' homework back to them, where it belongs.

Instead of the usual Post View section, I've substituted my Student Beatitudes and Student Commandments.

Student Beatitudes

1. Blessed is the student who turns in neat, legible homework, preferably in pen or #2 pencil, for his report-card grades will reflect his consideration of his teacher's eyesight. For she shall overlook many small errors when determining his grades.

2. Blessed is the student whose conduct is exemplary in the eyes of his teacher. For he shall receive extra privileges like taking notes to the office and cleaning the hamster cage.

3. Blessed is the student who exercises judicious restraint in confrontations with his teacher. For his parents shall smile when they see good conduct grades on his report card and perhaps be inclined to increase his allowance.

4. Blessed is the student who plans well ahead for his science project. For he shall receive school-and local-newspaper recognition, accolades from parents and teachers and maybe even from that "special" person in his class. He shall also be given lots of free time out of class for setting up his project for the Science Fair.

5. Blessed is the student who maintains a 4.0 GPA throughout high school, for he shall receive scholarship offers to prestigious universities and thereby contribute to the economic solvency of his parents.

6. Blessed is the student who does his homework within the prescribed parameters. For he shall reap the rewards of good grades and also prevent restriction of privileges, ear damage from parental rage, and maybe even loss of prized possessions.

7. Blessed is the student who remembers his lunch, his homework, and a miscellany of signed papers before leaving for school. For he shall not be embarrassed to see that the harried courier to his classroom, wearing hair rollers and no makeup, is his mother!

8. Blessed is the student who excels in some area, like character, personality, or behavior, despite an apparent lack of academic acumen. For his parents shall not entirely rue the day he was born.

9. Blessed is the student who remembers to give his father more than night-before notice that he volunteered him to speak to his class on World Banking. For he shall avoid the wrath of parentdom, subsequent gnashing of teeth, and high-decibel pronouncements of portending doom.

10. Blessed is the student who exercises good judgment in guarding the sanctity, privacy, and confidentiality of current events of home and hearth. For he shall discover that the "sharing" of such personal information as, "I don't have any brothers or sisters, because my mom had her tubes tied," will casually be relayed to his mom at the next parent-teacher conference. For he shall receive a dressing down not soon to be forgotten!

Student Commandments

1. Thou shalt not put pleasure before thy homework.

2. Thou shalt not make idols of TV, Nintendo, and sports.

3. Thou shalt not speak disrespectfully to thy teachers.

4. Thou shalt keep school evenings for thy homestudy.

5. Thou shalt try thy hardest to honor the achievement admonitions of thy parents.

6. Thou shalt not break thy parents' hearts by demonstrating disinterest in learning.

7. Thou shalt not break thy assignment commitments.

8. Neither shalt thou lie to thy parents about homework assignments.

9. Thou shalt not steal answers from thy classmates.

10. Thou shalt not covet grades that thou canst not earn for thyself, for thy best is all that is required.

8

Reaching for the Rs

*"The great thing in this world
is not so much where we are,
but in what direction we are moving."*

—OLIVER WENDELL HOLMES

*E*ducators say unequivocally that parent involvement sends a message to kids that outweighs other factors. If we want to turn our underachievers into achievers, we must not be tame, timid, or tepid when it comes to expectations for their achievement!

The purpose of this chapter is not to provide textbook level information or to turn parents into full-time teachers. Comprehensive instruction for your child remains the responsibility of his classroom teacher. What you will find here is information that you can use to increase your child's learning efficiency during his homestudy sessions.

Included in this information will be ideas, suggestions, and techniques for helping Billy and Susie learn how to think and study more effectively, as well as tips for memorizing, preparing for tests, and reducing test-taking stress. After using these teacher-approved ideas and suggestions, you'll see almost immediate improvement. In fact, their study sessions will be operating as efficiently as a satellite campus!

Parents, your first assignment for helping Billy and Susie reach for success in their own Rs is to ask the principal for a copy of the school district's grade-level continuum. This continuum lists the entry- or exit-level proficiencies expected for each grade. These proficiencies will become a checklist of objectives for Billy and Susie to master. Pick up your school's continuum today. You will find it helpful!

Next, make this promise to your child. "Billy/Susie, with me as your personal homework manager, from the neck up, there's absolutely no limit to what you can accomplish!"

Teaching Kids to Think

Why do we need to think? Why are our kids so "hard of thinking"? Who's responsible for this dearth of thinking? How can we improve thinking? These are fundamental questions that need to be answered before we can focus on the mastery techniques in specific subject areas.

One writer said that education in America is soft on thinking and hard on facts. With our present level of technology, computer-based systems can provide better than split-second retrieval of information. But computers don't think, not yet. People do. That's why it's important for our kids to know how to think, if they're to be prepared for a competitive future.

Why Do Our Kids Need to Think?

The *Wall Street Journal* of July 22, 1992, carried one of the most insightful articles I've ever read on what's wrong with education in America. It was written by Barbara Bronson Gray, parent of two and a part-time lecturer at the UCLA School of Nursing.

136

Gray cites several incidents in her own children's suburban school, where far too much school time is spent on the likes of picnics, amusement park field trips, and art projects. She points out that this school serves kids in a community where all kinds of extracurricular activities are already available and provided by most two-parent families earning annual, median incomes of $70,000!

Knowing how to think is increasingly important to our children and our country.

She continues by saying that far too little time is spent on instruction, correction, writing, and critical-thinking activities. Spelling and grammar papers come home uncorrected. Teachers claim too little time to correct and that correcting written work inhibits the creative process and lowers self-esteem. Classroom bulletin boards display, as exemplary, what resemble first-draft copies.

The usual book report requirements of remembering, summarizing, analyzing, and writing down what was read have been replaced in this school with making mobiles and dioramas to illustrate the book's concept. Is there any wonder that writing skills are among the weakest according to national tests?

Most of what is taught as writing today is creative writing, journal writing, and free expression. (Teachers will also tell you that this approach requires less instruction.) Structure, research, and argument techniques are considered old-fashioned, according to Gray.

She concluded that the problem in her children's school was not a problem of money, but a problem of complacency, a problem with one's philosophy of education, or a lack of understanding of what it's going to take for our kids to function as adults.

Knowing how to think is increasingly important to our children and our country. A professor in the U.S. recently gave a math problem from a Japanese college entrance exam to 350 freshman math students. It was a four-step problem that required the student to apply knowledge from each preceding step to solve the next step. Most Japanese students solved the problem. None of the American students could, and most of them couldn't even move to the second step! Our students were okay in computation but didn't have the math-thinking concepts to apply their computational skills.

So, why do our kids need to think? Because thinking is the foundation for developing the study skills that enable them to acquire and apply information.

Why Are Our Kids So Resistant to Thinking?

The short answer is because thinking is hard work, and most kids today are allergic to work, especially that of the mental variety. In case you haven't noticed, work is about as desirable to kids as last year's clothing fad. Give kids any assignment that requires thinking, applied reasoning, or problem-solving techniques, and rigorous resistance is guaranteed!

One education professor reported that U.S. public schools spend less than 1 percent of class time in discussions that require reasoning. In a National Commission report on Excellence in Education only one student in five could express a point of view and organize persuasive thoughts about it. Our kids simply do not wish to think, and, apparently, are not being required to do so!

Perhaps some educators erroneously believe that reasoning and thinking skills are inherent components of intelligence. Richard Paul, director of the Center for Critical Thinking, says kids can't even apply reasonable thought to everyday situations, like purchasing a bike. They are more likely to make their selection based on color or the type their friend has than they are to consider price, durability, or performance.

A Yale educational psychologist said lack of thinking skills can produce serious problems. He said youngsters who fail to learn how to measure the consequences of their actions may end up as drug abusers.

Finally, if we do everything for our kids, where is the incentive and motivation to do things for themselves, like thinking? That's why we must teach kids how to "reach for their own stars."

Who's Responsible for This Dearth of Thinking?

Instruction in critical thinking skills has been called "America's greatest educational neglect." This national level curricula void in our schools urgently needs our attention. Placing blame is a complicated task, because the educational, curricula, and instructional issues involved raise the ire, stir the emotions, and intrude into "hallowed" space reserved for academicians.

However, the finger of blame has been pointed in some familiar directions. Thinking requires effort, hard work, and perseverance, and these virtues have been *out* since the '60s and '70s. What was *in* was "doing your own thing," which didn't amount to much worth remembering.

The television industry—network moguls, writers, and advertisers—must accept some of the blame for our lack of thinking for producing programming that persuades and entices its viewers by saying: "Let us think for you, interpret the news and issues for you, set values and ethics for you, and, of course, entertain you. In short, let us perpetually keep your minds on 'autopilot' so long as our ratings are good!"

How Can We Improve Thinking?

One of the best ways you can help your child to improve his thinking skills is by asking questions, questions, and more questions. Thinking takes time. Don't hurry him for answers. This is one of the quickest turn-offs to thinking. If you're impatient, or your time is very limited, tell him to think about the answer and come back with it or tape it so you can listen later. Always get back to him after the listening, or he'll assume you really weren't interested in his answer.

Explore God's beautiful world with your kids; take nature walks, read and discuss good books with them; listen to good music; read poetry together; visit museums; look at the stars; and yes, even watch TV with them. But most of all, talk with them and ask lots of questions—*what if* questions; *why* questions; *how* questions. The *who, what, when, and where* questions do not require much thinking, only memory! You must move beyond these to be in the realm of critical or in-depth thinking.

When there is mutual respect for each member of the family, kids are more apt to contribute conversation, share their ideas, and discuss their daily activities.

Ask them to summarize what they read or watched; draw conclusions, predict outcomes, and infer meanings (read between the lines) from newspaper stories, books read, or TV shows. Ask them to imagine, create, condense, reword, explain the humor, etc.

Establish a respect for a thinking atmosphere at your house. Welcome conversation with your kids. Make and take time for it. One researcher reported that parents spend less than fifteen minutes a day in actual conversation with each child. Another researcher reported seven minutes! When there is mutual respect for each member of the family, kids are more apt to contribute conversation, share their ideas, and discuss their daily activities. Listen to your child talk so you can ask the questions that lead to critical thinking.

The dinner table is a great place to talk. Turn the TV off and have each member of the family share something that happened during the day: what he's learned, what's coming up, an unresolved issue, or some event that required thinking and decision making.

Engaging kids in conversation provides parents with the opportunity to assist kids in speaking more clearly and precisely.

Imprecise speaking is the cause of misunderstanding. Kids use careless phrases in informal conversation, and their writing skills reflect this same carelessness. When kids learn to speak in clearly understood sentences, they also write less ambiguously.

When what they say is not making sense, ask for clarification like this: "Do you really mean. . . .? But you said. . . . Do you see how you could be misunderstood by the way you said it? Oh, now I understand; that's much more clear."

Ask them to explore the other person's point of view, evaluate the pros and cons of a problem or issue, and measure good and bad points prior to making decisions. This skill is important in developing relationships, resolving problems, and making decisions throughout their lives.

Without a knowledge base, most of our thoughts would not be worth the paper to record them. Most extemporaneous or shallow thinkers couldn't hold their own for two minutes in a debate. Only experts in their fields are able to speak extemporaneously, and that's because they've already internalized a knowledge base in their particular field.

Thinking is not a substitute for study, which is necessary for acquiring knowledge and information. And knowledge is not a substitute for thinking when new situations call for decision making. Most kids offer quick answers without really thinking, which demonstrates mental lethargy!

For an example of what I mean, pose the following questions of little Billy. "How do you spell, *host?*" Wait for his answer. Then, "How do you spell, *most? How do you spell, *coast? How do you spell what you put in a *toaster?*"

If he's an extemporaneous thinker and hasn't heard the riddle before, he'll most likely spell, "T-o-a-s-t." Of course, the thinker's answer is, *"B-r-e-a-d,"* for bread is what you put in the toaster. It comes out as *toast.*

With the thinking issue behind us, in the next section I'd like to share some "insider tips" from teachers. These memory techniques and study tips will enable your kids not only to recall the information they've gathered, but also pass tests, and impress their teachers in classroom discussions!

Insider Tips:
Mnemonics, Highlighters, and Learning Expediters

Mnemonics (Memory Techniques)

From one study it was reported that kids could recall the names of 4.8 presidents and 5.2 beers! It appears that advertisers may know more about memory than educators. Maybe educators need to be a little less pedagogical and a lot more practical in teaching kids ways to remember what they learn.

The hippocampus area of the brain is the location of our mental archives. Brain researchers have found a layer of 4.6 million cells in this area, believed to be the processing plant for new facts before they are sent out for storage elsewhere.

From one study it was reported that kids could recall the names of 4.8 presidents and 5.2 beers!

One psychobiologist referred to this area as the "black hole" because brain researchers are still trying to discover how the mind can store an estimated 100 trillion bits of information. This file system boggles the mind when we compare the computer's ability to store only mere billions. Of course, what many parents are wondering is why their child can't remember the spelling words for Friday's test!

Mnemonics are defined as methods to assist memory. Samuel Johnson called memory "the art of attention." And memory researchers tell us if we pay attention, we can improve our memories up to 50 percent!

Memory is improved by seeing relationships, finding differences, and doing in-depth thinking. We're not asking or expecting Billy and Susie to become "Memory Mozarts," which is what one psychologist called those with superior memories. For example, music conductor Arturo Toscanini memorized every note for every instrument in 100 operas and 250 symphonies!

Most of us are able to recall only one out of every one hundred bits of information we receive daily. Therefore, if we want our kids' retention to improve, we must teach them how to enrich their memories by saturating the storage process. According to memory experts, when we thoroughly learn something our brains create many neural pathways leading back to the stored information. In other words, we create a cross-indexing system for remembering things.

This cross-indexing system is a result of learning to use basically three types of memory techniques: relational, visual, and sequential. Kids can learn to use each of these; and they can also be combined, thereby strengthening the brain's cross-referencing system.

Relational. Use this memory technique to recall a list of related items to be learned. One author gives this example for memorizing the names of the planets by making up a silly sentence with the first letter of each word as a clue to recall each planet in order.

"My very excellent mother just served us nine pizzas."

Having your child make up his own personalized, relational sentence is best, because he is required to concentrate.

Visual. Kids seem to be less able to use the visualization technique than the other ones. This difficulty may be the result of busy parents having less time to spend reading and telling stories to their youngsters. These activities provide early development of a child's visualization skills.

One example of the visualization technique is remembering names by linking the name with a visual rhyme or by visualizing the person performing an activity similar to the sound of the name. For example, to remember the name Jerry, visualize him taking a ferry; or Arthur, authoring a book.

Sequential. Facts to be learned that have a logical order lend themselves to the sequential mnemonics. This technique is frequently combined with one of the others. For example, in order to recall the events in a story, they are more easily recalled if the child visualizes the place and sequence of the events as they occurred in the story.

Learning Expediters

All learning does not take place while sitting at a desk with a sharpened #2 pencil in hand. Let's look at some tips, techniques, and technologies that make the most of available time and resources.

Travel-Study Bags

It's been estimated that we spend six years of our lives eating, five years waiting in lines, and six months at red lights, doctors' offices, banks, etc. This estimate overlooks one of the biggest unused resources of time—time spent in cars, buses, and planes!

Thomas Edison said, "Everything comes to him who hustles while he waits." Kids spend lots of time waiting, too. One way to make the best of "down time" is to see that Billy and Susie have their travel-study bags packed at all times. These need to be ready to grab at a moment's notice as you're dashing out the door to do errands, run to the bank, or for a doctor's appointment. If you have to wait for them to find and pack their study stuff, you may as well forget it. It takes too much time.

Be sure their travel-study bags include the essentials: note pad, paper, pencil, pen, highlighters, index cards, and the current priority study materials. Here are some activities that are appropriate for short study sessions:

- Practice spelling words.
- Study vocabulary cards.
- Study math flash cards.
- Read for an upcoming book report.
- Read an assigned chapter in a text.
- Study notes for an upcoming test.
- Draft an outline for an upcoming project.
- Correct errors on returned homework assignments.

Parents, remember that teachers don't give grades for studying hard or studying longer. But kids' grades will reflect whether or not they've learned to study smart.

Studying, Test-Taking, and Memorizing

Doctors, psychologists, and educators say the following general suggestions will contribute to smart studying:

1. Eat a snack that includes protein approximately one hour before studying or taking tests. Protein provides "brain" food. Eating candy, sweet rolls, donuts, sugar-coated cereals, etc. can cause the blood sugar to drop within an hour and produce a sluggish student.
2. Study in short bursts. Six twenty-minute sessions are better than one two-hour session.
3. The first and last things studied are the easiest to recall.
4. Playing thinking games like chess and Jeopardy, and working with puzzles have been shown to raise the IQ by 5 points! There's some new data indicating listening to classical music shows similar results.
5. To increase concentration, try running, doing push-ups, jumping rope, and deep breathing prior to studying, or at twenty-minute intervals during study.
6. Tape difficult lectures for review before tests.
7. Study right up to the classroom door for the best test results.
8. Approach test-taking with a contest spirit, positive attitude, and a preset grade goal!
9. Study hard stuff first, easy stuff last.
10. Use multisensory mnemonics: See it, say it, feel it, sing it, write it, and even highlight the difficult areas for last-minute review.

Computer-Assisted Instruction

Computers have to be among the top ten discoveries of the twentieth century. They're used everywhere: in business, science, industry, communication, law enforcement, and, at last, in education! They've become indispensable tools. Employers increasingly demand computer literacy, and knowledge of computers and software programs definitely gives the prospective employee a hiring advantage.

From an educator's point of view, kids who have computers, or at least know how to use them, have a number of distinct advantages. Computer software is available for just about any subject and for all grade levels. If at all possible, see that your child has use of a computer. CAUTION: Before purchasing a computer, check out what educational software is available for the one you plan to buy. If there is little or no educational software, the computer is little more than an expensive paperweight or toy.

Here are just some of the educational advantages computers offer:

1. Computers are great for drill and practice.
2. Kids learn from a gaming format.
3. The software is self-teaching, self-correcting, and self-pacing.
4. Computer software uses high-interest, exciting, color graphics that kids love!
5. Kids can learn and use word processing, which is an incredible advantage for writing and editing essays and research papers.
6. Computers are very patient tutors, and there are some great software programs for just about every school subject and for all grade levels.
7. With the new interactive technology, a world of knowledge is a key pad away!

See Billy and Susie Excel!

*"Any subject can be taught effectively
in some intellectually honest form
to any child at any stage of development."*
—JEROME S. BRUNER

*I*n this last chapter you will find tips and techniques that you as homestudy managers can use in helping your child reach new heights of achievement in specific subject or topic areas. You may wish to concentrate on those areas that pertain to your own child.

Mastery

No matter what needs to be learned—names, dates, problems, products, presidents, rivers, continents, math facts, spelling words, or definitions —the following KWL technique is a process that will help to clarify what it is that the child already knows and what needs to be learned. This knowledge alone helps to reduce the "tedium and trauma" of mastering material.

Teachers have been training students to use KWL or a variation for nearly a half century. In fact, KWL works for any learning that lends itself to rote memory. I suggest using index cards, because cards are not only durable and packable in his travel-study bag, but Billy can shuffle and sort the cards into *known* and *learn* sets following the KWL plan, i.e.:

K = What I *know* already.
W = What I *want to learn*
L = What I *learned.*

Language Arts

Reading and Phonics

It's commonly reported that television news anchors make millions of dollars annually, and some would argue that their primary job description is to read teleprompters effectively! So, if your kids are motivated by money, this fact just might be the push needed.

On a more serious note, there's probably no other area that causes greater concern for parents than having a child who isn't learning to read according to his ability expectations. For most kids, learning to read is anticipated with excitement and enthusiasm. Unfortunately, for others, reading is a dreaded and fearful task.

Because the English language is 85 percent phonetically decoded and the remaining 15 percent partially phonetic, learning to read should not cause such anxiety. Japanese children must know between five thousand and nine thousand characters to be able to read at third-grade level, and Chinese children must learn some thirty-five hundred characters to read very simple books. Well-educated adults must learn some 1,850,000 characters. So, let's not feel sorry for Billy, who needs to master only forty-four sound-symbol relationships in order to read close to a million English words!

Phonics works 99.44 percent of the time with normal kids— if there's phonics mastery!

For example, an analysis of seven thousand English words showed that correct spelling patterns can be predicted for letter-sound relationships 90 percent of the time when basic phonetic facts are taken into consideration. I'm very aware of the educational debate and dialogue about which is the best approach for teaching reading. My doctoral research and dissertation were both in the area of reading. But, trust me, as a teacher, reading clinician, and published researcher on the topic, phonics works 99.44 percent of the time with normal kids—if there's phonics mastery!

And remember, beginning readers don't really have that many words to master in order to learn to read. Take a look at the following word-frequency facts in reading materials:

- 100 words make up 60 percent of elementary reading;
- 500 words make up 82 percent of elementary reading;
- 1000 words make up 89 percent of elementary reading;
- 2000 words make up 95 percent of elementary reading.

These word-frequency facts alone suggest that if you want to give your child a head start in reading, have him memorize the basic sight words from the Common Word List of the most frequently used words. You'll find a copy of the Common Word List in Appendix A. Have him master five new words a day from this list! "Mastery" means he can pronounce them at the rate of one word per second. Another advantage of having the child memorize these common words is that these words contain many of the phonetic exceptions. So, have him learn these words as sight words.

If your Billy is not learning to read as quickly as you or his teacher expects, try the following steps. In six short weeks, I promise you that his progress will astound you.

Step 1. Ask your child's teacher to get you a supplementary or discarded reader for his grade level so he can do the following activity.

Step 2. Turn to Appendix C and find the Super Sleuth phonic perception sheet. Make about twenty-five photocopies.

Step 3. Have him master the Read Right Away (RRA) phonic information, sets #1-10, provided in Appendix B. Play phonics mastery fifteen to thirty minutes a day, and he will learn them in about two weeks.

Step 4. In his (discarded copy) grade-level reader, using highlighters, have him do the following daily, for six weeks:

- Find all of the Vowels + R (Read Right Away Set #3) on one page. Highlight all of them, using *one* color highlighter.
- Find all of the "H" Family (RRA Set #4) on *another* page. Highlight all of them, using a different color highlighter.
- Find all of the Vowel Combinations (RRA Set #10) on *another* page. Highlight all of them, using yet another color highlighter.
- Parents, you can make this activity into a game by counting the number of each of the phonic parts to be highlighted on each page. The child tries to match his phonic-perception ability with yours. If he gets 100 percent (or progressively very close), reward him in some appropriate way.

Step 5. If a supplementary or discarded grade-level reader is not available, use the photocopies of Super Sleuth perception sheets found in Appendix C for this activity. The child writes the phonic parts found on each page instead of highlighting them in a book. This procedure is more time consuming but is actually even more effective because it involves both visual and tactile senses.

Step 6. Each day, have him read the same three pages aloud to you on which he did his highlighting or Super Sleuthing. See that he highlights and reads aloud three different pages each day. Set a goal of no more than three word errors per page. Keep a daily record of the number of errors, so he can see his progress toward reading accuracy.

Step 7. Have him master five words a day from the Common Word List discussed earlier. The list can be found in Appendix A.

Step 8. If your child is in fourth grade or above, have him master RRA Set #16 and be familiar with Sets #11-15 as well. This information will enable him to approach more difficult words with less fear. As he learns how to "divide and conquer" longer words, these small successes will lead to increased confidence in his own independent decoding skills.

General Reading Suggestions

For every hour Billy and Susie watch TV, they must read for pleasure that same amount of time! Develop a "TV Watch Punch Card" for record keeping.

Ask your city or school librarian to provide you with a list of the most popular books, such as the Newberry Award-winning books. See that some of the age-grade appropriate ones are always available at home in your child's interest level. And last, but not the least in importance, your child should see you reading as much as you watch TV!

Spelling

Misspelled, mispronounced, and misused words are like flaws in a diamond or ink spots on white shirts. Model and expect your child to be precise in his use and spelling of words. His teachers grade him by the way he speaks, writes, and spells.

Kids learn to read before they learn to spell. This is a logical progression because reading is actually easier than spelling. This truism probably has something to do with the whole-and-sum-of-its-parts thing. For example, a child recognizes people and things long before he can describe them in detail, from memory. If your child is not a good speller, the following procedure promises to turn most normal children into excellent spellers.

1. See the word carefully.
2. Say the word clearly *by syllable*.
3. "Silly-Say" the word as it is spelled, if the word is only partially phonetic. For example, Pronounce the word *colonel* as *co-lo-nel*.
4. Color-code-clue words with double letters, silent letters, or other obvious non-phonetic trouble spots.
5. Write the words from dictation.
6. Highlight the letter-error misspellings. This step is very important, because it minimizes the problem area within each word misspelled.
7. Repeat #5 and #6 until all words can be correctly spelled from *one* dictation.
8. State that you expect him to get 100 percent on his spelling tests.

Syllabication and Word Busters

For fun, practice, and improved spelling and reading, play Word Busters with your child! I developed this game when I was teaching. All students 4th grade and above enjoyed it. Even junior-high students begged to play it! Dividing words into syllables is fun when it has a gaming format. Rules and scoring directions are found on the bottom of the Word Buster player sheet found in Appendix D.(Better Xerox many copies!)

Before playing Word Busters, your child (4th grade or above) must learn the seven rules for splitting words into syllables. See RRA Set #16 in Appendix B for these rules.

Stress-Free Comprehension

Studies have shown that kids spend about 70 percent of their time in school filling in blanks on worksheets and too much time on skills and drills. The result is that kids end up with no general comprehension ability. Poor comprehension problems are even more common than illiteracy. Even though Billy and Susie can read, steps must be taken to ensure that they comprehend what they read.

For years I've been encouraging teachers in my Stress-Free Comprehension Workshops to cut the tethers to their textbooks and opt for "dittoless" Fridays. I challenge them to spend some of this time in class discussion about how to detect what's important in whole chapters or books their students have read, and discussing how to take notes. I call this teaching "global comprehension."

Since all authors of textbooks develop their texts in some order, it's also very helpful for kids, at least by fourth or fifth grade, to be familiar with the author's textbook structure. There are four patterns of textbook structure that have been identified: simple listing, time order, cause-effect, and comparison-contrast. Once a child understands how his textbook is organized, he is better able to use it, find answers to chapter questions, and generally understand its content.

One frequently-used study technique for teaching kids how to read and study textbook material is called SQR-3. This technique lends itself specifically to comprehensive, historical, or conceptual material found in history, social studies, geography, and literature texts. SQR-3 involves the following steps:

Survey. The child surveys (reads quickly) chapter headings and subheadings, introduction and summary sections, end-of-chapter questions, and vocabulary lists. This survey provides the student with the chapter's "big picture," and is sometimes referred to as the preread.

Question. From the chapter headings and subheadings kids make up their own questions to which they expect to find answers as they read.

Read. Kids then read the entire chapter, trying to answer the questions they've asked that relate back to the various topics.

Recite. What students read is understood and remembered longer if they talk about its content and take notes.

Review. The final step is for the child to review his notes and the questions he made up, as well as the author's questions at the end of the chapter.

Mind-Mapping and Note-Taking

Another, and my favorite, technique that improves global comprehension and teaches note-taking at the same time is called "mind-mapping." Briefly stated, mind-mapping is taking notes that catch the mind's attention as the child reads, listens to his teacher, or views a film. Mind-mapping is recorded on regular notebook paper rather than index cards. Cards provide too little surface space for drawing the entire mind map on one card. Mind maps allow kids to be creative and artistic, and at the same time, reduce some of the stigma attached to note-taking. Most kids like making mind maps because they're generally more creative than they are adept at taking notes. A few samples of Mind Maps are included for various ages and subjects in Appendix E. In addition, some mnemonic reminders that will enable your child to be a better mind mapper are listed here:

1. The brain's storage system is precise. Give it clear and concise information bits, not paragraphs, for it to store. Do not use complete sentences in mind maps.
2. The brain recalls more efficiently big, bold, and neat bits of information. Don't do messy maps and don't crowd your words.
3. The brain remembers what it sees in color up to four times over what it sees in black and white. Use colored highlighters to code the most important points to remember.

Reducing Test-Taking Stress

I've found the best thing to reduce test-taking stress is learning something well. This may not sound profound enough to impress my colleagues, but I don't see kids who experience stress or have difficulty recalling what they've really learned well.

Stress that is the result of extreme or prolonged trauma can indeed block memory, but in most cases related to test taking, it's not the test that's creating the stress. It's that the material was not learned to begin with, and the brain knows it. In fact, stress is the way in which the brain sends a message to Billy. "Hey, Billy! You're in trouble, *big time,* 'cause you don't know this stuff yet!"

So, my simple remedy for reducing test-taking stress is to make sure your child can respond with information, facts, vocabulary definitions, etc., without hesitation and stammering. In short, his response time starts within one-second—the same time that it takes to tell you his name!

Here are a few final suggestions commonly reported as beneficial for reducing academic-related stress:

Stress-Reduction Tips

1. Be positive, firm, and realistic about your child's grade expectations, based upon his age, ability, gifts, and limitations.
2. Recognize your child's non-academic strengths, and help him to develop his own particular interests and unique talents, whatever they be.
3. Always focus on his progress toward his goal, as well as the achievement of his goal. When he improves from 80 percent to 93 percent, and his goal was 98 percent, that's quality progress!
4. Validate his worth as an individual when he's having a problem, and offer assistance in working together with him to ameliorate or resolve the problem.

Written Compositions

In comprehending and completing written reports, teachers report that students have the greatest difficulty in seeing the *preview* or *overview* of a composition assignment. Be it a book report, topical essay, or research paper, here are some "management" tips for parents to use the next time your child brings home that "dreaded" writing assignment.

Book Reports

Most teachers who require book reports have their own preferred structure and outline requirements for students to use. However, most all book-reports include these basic components: title, author, setting, main characters, favorite or main character descriptions, and a brief story overview.

Here are some suggestions for taking the pain out of making book reports:

1. Be sure he indeed reads the book. Any experienced teacher can smell a bluff book report a mile away.
2. Using basic math, have him figure out how many pages a day he must read in order to finish his book at least one week before the book report is due. Following this plan allows adequate time for several drafts of his report.
3. Have him treat each item in his book report outline as a question. Have him use a separate note card for each question and answer each question as he reads. When he's finished reading, he has the first draft of his book report.
4. Have him translate his cards and answered questions into complete sentences. Follow the Basic Seven Checklist below, and voila, he has the final draft of his book report!

Did you . . .

_____ 1. use complete sentences?

_____ 2. begin each sentence with a capital?

_____ 3. end your sentences with punctuation?

_____ 4. check the spelling of difficult words?

_____ 5. use an apostrophe in words showing possession?

_____ 6. follow the assignment guidelines?

_____ 7. use your "neatness" skills?

Review Billy's first, second, or however many drafts it takes, of his book report. Give him the appropriate compliments and necessary reminders, like: "That's a pretty good first draft. But if you want to save time on redrafting, you better take a look at # 2 and # 4 on your Basic 7 Checklist before starting your next draft."

Topic Essays/Research Papers

Students always have considered essays and research papers to be among the most rigorous and least desirable assignments a teacher gives. Writing good essays and research papers requires three necessary steps: (1) determine what questions need to be answered; (2) select the resource materials needed to answer these questions; (3) develop an outline for presenting and sequencing the material gathered.

In case the teacher doesn't provide the research questions or the format to be followed, here's a basic outline to use, including some suggestions regarding the content for each section and the approximate space to be allotted each section.

Introduction. State the purpose and scope of the paper in this section. (Approximately one paragraph.)

Need or Problem. The problem is stated clearly, and several authorities in the particular field should be quoted or paraphrased to corroborate the problem and a need for its resolution. (One page.)

Background and Issues. This is sometimes called the "body" of the research paper. This is the section in which the student answers the proposed research questions and presents information from his review of periodicals, magazines, encyclopedias, etc., regarding the issues surrounding the research topic. (Approximately two pages per question or issue.)

Summary. In this section, briefly bring together the key points from each question or issue from the body of the paper. (One-half page.)

Conclusions. Here, the student presents what he has learned or what has been concluded by others concerning his topic or research subject. (One or two paragraphs.)

Suggestions. This component in research papers is usually required of more sophisticated high-school or college-level students. In this section, the student states the need for gathering more information, or suggests some changes in the way in which any future research is done. (One-half page.)

Format and Presentation

Designers, decorators, and advertisers alike know that the motivation to buy cars, houses, clothes, or food items is based in part upon eye appeal. This is also true when teachers have their pens poised, ready to make their grade decisions. So don't let Billy and Susie forget for one moment that eye appeal is also a real factor in their letter grades. Neatness is evidence of a student's pride in his work!

Grammar

Grammar is a precise, complex subject to teach; and my advice to parents is to leave grammar instruction up to the teacher. However, if parents feel "grammar confident," they might review their child's grammar homework assignment, highlight the errors, and remind him to review his textbook examples before making corrections.

One of my teacher friends developed this little song as a quick way to help her students learn the parts of speech. You may find it helpful.

Planet Grammar

Words by Shirley Moffitt
(To the tune, "Do-re-mi," from The Sound of Music)

I'm a Noun, a per-son, place, or thing.
I'm Pro-noun; I take NOUN'S place.
I'm Con-junc-tion; I con-nect.
I'm Ad-verb; I modify.
I'm Ad-jec-tive, and I de-scribe.
I'm an In-ter-jec-tion, Whee! Oh! My!
I'm a Verb; I tell what ac-tion is.
Pre-po-si-tion? "ON" the Pla-net Gram-mar.
G - R - A - M - M - A - R
G - R - A - M - M - A - R
When you know the parts of speech,
Pla-net Gram-mar you may reach!

Math Systems

If test scores across the country are any indication, America needs achievers in all areas, but especially in math and science. Although all students will not become mathematicians or have Einsteinian aspirations, they all will need to understand and use numbers!

Because teachers are the instructional experts, let them teach kids the math concepts. What teachers would appreciate is parents' assistance in making sure that their youngsters master the basic math facts. Once they've mastered addition, subtraction, multiplication, division, weights and measures, fractions, decimals, and percentages, parents can be sure their kids at least have the math foundation that prepares them to understand higher math-level concepts.

Math Flash Cards

First through fourth graders are learning to master the basic addition, subtraction, multiplication, and division facts. For efficient mastery of the basic math facts, flash cards are hard to beat. Since all higher levels of math have these facts as their foundation, it's imperative that your child knows these facts in a flash!

What's so great about flash cards? To name a few: they're on durable card stock; numbers are big, bold, and colorful; they're sortable into appropriate stacks of what's known and what's not (KWL); and the answers are on the back of each card, which makes them self-teaching and self-correcting! (I did have one client who brought math flash cards that had the answers on the same side as the math problem! Avoid this type.)

Here are five points to remember about using math flash cards:

1. Establish the Mastery Objective: Billy will master five new math facts a day. Responses are to be within one second. Proof of mastery rewards him with a regular meal ticket instead of the Veggie Menu! (See Appendix F)
2. Once you have quizzed your child on his daily mastery of math facts, you initial the upper righthand corner of the flash card. This way, he always knows which ones he knows and which ones he doesn't. This is important because most all flash cards are two-sided, and it's confusing as to which ones he has mastered unless you initial the ones already learned.
3. Mastery "maintenance" must be monitored. Each time you quiz him, be sure to use all the initialed cards plus the five new ones. Daily math fact drills will ensure that he maintains the previously learned facts.
4. Work on only one math concept at a time, following this sequence: addition, subtraction, multiplication, and division, until he can do one hundred math facts in five minutes or less, with 98 percent accuracy! His teacher can provide you with math worksheets to use. Make extra photocopies as needed.

5. Highlight his errors on his math worksheets. Then put an identifying mark (like MP for "more practice") that indicates these flash cards are not yet at mastery level.

Attention all parent math managers! One study reported a 20 percent increase in math grades when kids wrote numbers clearly, aligned their number columns precisely, copied problems correctly, attended class regularly, and sat in the front row.

Weights and Measures

It's impossible for a child to do well in math if he doesn't know simple weight and measurement facts. Find out from his teacher what he is supposed to know. Put this information on index cards. Use hands-on manipulatives that you've made or purchased at a teachers' supply store. Draw or cut out picture examples and glue-stick them to the back of his cards. Put the "fact" question on the front of the card. Bottom line, see that he learns them ASAP, making use of his smart-study time!

Fractions, Decimals, and Percentages

The same procedure given for weights and measures applies here. Kids cannot excel in math beyond about third-grade level without understanding the concepts of fractions, decimals, and percents.

Today's math workbooks have great, colorful graphics. Cut out the ones that represent problem areas and paste them on index cards for memory and practice. Concepts, of course, need to be understood first, but those who understand the concepts far outweigh those who actually master the facts. Knowledge of the concepts without fact mastery promises one thing: Billy and Susie will continue to fail math tests! They must be able to apply both concept knowledge and facts if they are to work efficiently and accurately at test time. Generally, it's not really a matter of math-test stress, but lack of math-fact mastery that creates the stress!

Making Math Relevant

Educators urge parents to use every practical opportunity to make math relevant to kids. Here are a few ideas plus a couple of suggested books full of ideas and activities for making math relevant: Show your child how to:

1. Budget his allowance.
2. Figure and compare the costs of toys, games, clothes, gifts, grocery items, fast foods, etc.
3. Figure distances.
4. Measure areas for building projects, carpeting, painting the house.
5. Pay bills, write checks (Parents do the signing!), figure interest.
6. Use fractions, weights, and measures in cooking.

Math Resource Books

Family Math, University of California, EQUALS PROJECT, Lawrence Hall of Science. 318 pages of math activities for kids five to eighteen years of age, for parents and teachers.

Math Activities for Child Involvement, 4th Edition, C.W. Schminke, for four to sixteen years of age, four hundred stimulating math activities.

Science

America needs to be generating budding new scientists. And kids need science in order to learn about themselves, the universe, its inhabitants, and the environment.

But far too many science teachers are teaching outside their college major or minor fields. Therefore, they feel extremely uncomfortable teaching science, according to Nobel Laureate in Physics, Leon Lederman. He says that teachers can't teach science because they're terrified of it.

To make matters worse, science has earned the unfortunate reputation among kids as a low-interest, difficult, dry, vocabulary-memorizing subject. It's been reported that 50 percent of kids are turned off to science by age nine. This is because teachers are teaching about science rather than using a hands-on approach, which is the only real way to ignite kids' interest in science.

Writers of science textbooks know that terrified teachers who are non-science majors will be using their textbooks in classrooms with no lab equipment or the experience to use it. Based upon this information, the science textbook authors write textbooks and teaching manuals that more or less force teachers to teach about science. In the United States, it's very unusual to find a science teacher below the high-school or college level using a hands-on approach for teaching science.

Also, there's the *fog index,* or vocabulary level, of high-school science texts, which on an average has been estimated as equal to a first-year foreign language course! Kids are being asked to memorize twenty-four hundred to three thousand new terms! One student said, "Science texts are like dictionaries, and who wants to study a dictionary?"

Another problem unique to the subject of science pertains to the two opposing theories about the origin of man: evolution vs. creation. Parents will want to ensure that the textbook and teacher present both sides as viewpoints held by millions. Particularly, watch that your children's science grades do not reflect penalties given for not believing that man evolved from animals!

You may think that my suggestions for monitoring your child's science achievement are not too scientific, maybe even a tad extreme. They are:

1. Attend your school district's board meetings and your child's school PTA meetings, and voice loud and clear your concerns about your child's science instruction. Insist upon the use of films, experiments, demonstrations, field trips, guest speakers, and equal presentation of both theories of creation.
2. Help Billy and Susie apply all their study and comprehension skills, mnemonic techniques, and the vocabulary flash card suggestions given. They're going to need them in order to master their science book "dictionary."
3. Seek out a science "mentor" from the business community to ensure that your child sees the exciting and real-life applications of scientific principles.

4. Enroll Billy and Susie in a science-related community college summer programs for kids. These courses provide excellent enrichment activities.

Epilogue

1. Raising orchids is easier than raising kids.
2. Self-esteem grows as the child does, becomes, and knows.
3. The under-motivated do whatever is tolerated by parents. Where there's achievement resistance, there's probably parental inconsistence.
4. Tutorial remediation is the shortest road to acceleration; and when achievement is not happening, the consequences need tightening.
5. When little Billy And Susie play "Dumbo," it's time to "Spice up their gumbo!" Fifth grade and can't do fractions? It's time to "contract for action."
6. "Disuse is brain abuse!" America's kids suffer from intellect neglect and become even less enabled when labeled "disabled."
7. Billy and Susie should earn their mortar board and tassel without parents having the homework hassle.
8. Teach kids how to think instead of rescuing them from every brink.
9. When a parent sees their little Billy and Susie excel, pride begins to swell.

It's always gratifying to hear success stories when good things begin to happen with children, especially those who've had a history of school failure. So take a moment to drop me a note about your child's successes and your increased parenting confidence, along with some problems you're still working on. I like a challenge!

PART THREE

Appendices

Appendix A
Common Words Lists

This common-word list comprises the most frequently-used words from basal readers in first through third grades. Children should learn five new words a day from this list as sight words. Mastery level is reached when the child can recite one word per second!

Level One

after	on	can	before	pretty	
big	so	go	down	we	to
eat	to	I	of	red	you
had	and	make	six	the	your
its	brown	me	today	when	here
four	my	one	round	little	fix
her	at	once	then	his	today
like	cold	some	white	myself	all
are	going	under	who	not	black
but	if	or	run	do	fly
from	in	does	what	soon	he
around	up	into	want	that	jump
by	is	out	then	will	old
funny	it	gave	said	see	too
him	no	give	they	she	sleep
long	away	stop	night	an	as
come	walk	saw	I'll	blue	call

good	play	this	dog	for	get
green	laugh	yellow	boy	help	look
be	ten	three	sleep	just	ask
did	was	yes	why	many	other

Level Two

their	grow	wish	pick	over	only	drink
those	light	take	small	am	about	has
keep	both	there	could	done	now	warm
where	right	clean	use	work	with	full
far	eight	upon	many	came	tell	start
seven	fall	ran	goes	put	first	open
don't	may	live	bring	been	any	again
best	sing	by	made	much	new	us
were	got	say	says	own	every	off
gave	which	read	well	cut	try	these
how	have	would	sit	good	pull	should
five	our	draw	does	carry	let	know
it's	what's	that's	didn't	won't	let's	you'd
taught	caught	bought	hurt	fight	night	enough
rough	tough	always	better	thank	think	together
gone	never	please	because	write	began	before
must	hot	well	went	show	very	hold

fast   wash   kind   shall   ate   I'd   cough

find   begin   none   could   would   should   eat

Level Three—Common Nouns

cow	corn	ring	rabbit	coat	cat	Christmas
shoe	apple	kitten	back	doll	house	sheep
snow	aunt	bed	egg	bear	letter	duck
mother	baby	father	fish	goat	squirrel	boat
fire	boy	stork	sun	paper	game	night
car	thing	floor	nest	bird	farm	men
home	day	seed	horse	dog	money	school
way	tree	chair	girl	table	chicken	cake
time	box	night	water	top	flower	party
watch	wind	wood	hill	bell	eye	man
song	morning	milk	farmer	feet	street	bread
grass	ground	water	rain	children	robin	good-bye
toy	pig	head	hand	clothes	table	hunger
book	fall	summer	winter	animal	spring	tomatoes
July	postman	June	horse	airplane	tonight	January
March	April	August	baseball	present	pumpkin	December
May	telephone	teacher	fireman	February	weather	September

wish   evening lunch   dinner   October someone November

spoon   knife   fork   supper   sister   thought friend

ten   thirty   twenty   though hundred seventy ninety

sixty   fifty   anyone eighty   something minute addition

through brother forty   uncle   subtraction   arithmetic

Appendix B
Read Right Away

Read Right Away

© Nita Weis, Ph.D., 1960

Revised 1984, 1987, 1994

READ RIGHT AWAY consists of 16 Sets of phonetic information and 5 Drills. No attempt has been made to cover EVERY SOUND in the English language. However, the sequential mastery of the information provided here will enable the learner to acquire the independent decoding skills needed for reading most of the words in the English language.

Suggested use of the the READ RIGHT AWAY cards is as follows:

Kindergarten= A, B & Sets 1-8

First-Third = A, B & Sets 1-10

Fourth-Adult = A, B & Sets 1-16

A. ALPHABET RECOGNITION

UPPER CASE ALPHABET

B D F <u>E</u> G <u>A</u> C <u>I</u> <u>O</u> T X

Q Y P L N J M S Z II K

R V <u>U</u> W

LOWER CASE ALPHABET

w <u>u</u> v r k h z s m j n l p

y q x t <u>o</u> <u>i</u> c <u>a</u> <u>e</u> g f d b

---

1. Recognize out of order and name quickly all letters, both upper and lower case.

2. Know which letters are VOWELS and which are CONSONANTS.

3. Name the VOWELS from memory.
   (Vowels are underlined.)

4. W & Y are also vowels, sometimes.

5. Give the sounds of the CONSONANTS.

181

B. CONSONANT BLENDS

st	sk	tr	gr	sm	pl	br
cl	bl	dr	fr	sl	spr	sn
sc	dw	cr	pr	wr	fl	shr
	spl	scr	squ	str	gl	sp
tw	sw	ld	rf	rb	rk	mp
nt	rl	ck	rt	nd	rd	nk
		pt	lk	ct	ft	

1. Pronounce one blend per second.

SET 1. SHORT VOWEL SOUNDS

Ă = APPLE

Ĕ = EGG

Ĭ = INDIAN

Ŏ = OCTOPUS

Ŭ = UMBRELLA

1. Practice giving the short vowel sounds, out of order and quickly.

2. Memorize the "crutch" words for SHORT VOWELS.

NOTE:
In approximately 85% of the words in the English language, VOWELS will have the SHORT sound!

SET 2. LONG VOWEL RULES

1. ĀTE̸   =   Magic "E" on the end of words
makes the closest vowel LONG.

2. BŌA̸T   =   2 vowels together,
1st is LONG; 2nd is SILENT.

3. CŌLD   =   "O" and "I" are usually LONG when
   KĪND   followed by 2 CONSONANTS in
1 SYLLABLE words

4. PĀ́PER   =   When a vowel is on the END of an
ACCENTED SYLLABLE,
it is usually LONG.

---

1. Know and understand LONG VOWEL rules.

NOTE:

In approximately 15 percent of the words in the English language, VOWELS are LONG.

SET 3. VOWELS + "R"

AR = CAR (R)

* ER = HER

* IR = DIRT

OR = FORK

* UR = FUR

---

1. Give the VOWEL + R sounds out of order, quickly.

2. * Spell the three Vowels + R that have the same sound: ER - IR - UR.

3. Never divide Vowels + R when dividing words into syllables.

SET 4. THE " H " FAMILY

TH = THUMB

SH = SHIP

CH^3 = CHURCH (CH) most common sound
*   CHRISTMAS (K)
           MACHINE (SH)

WH = WHEEL

PH = (F) as in PHONE

GH^3 = GHOST (GUH) beginning of word
           TAUGHT (no sound) middle of word
           LAUGH (F) end of word
           (G - Ø - F)

---

1. Say "H" Family sounds out of order, quickly.

2. *CH followed by "R" or "L" always says "K."

3. Never divide the "H" Family when dividing words into syllables.

SET 5. "C" HAS 2 SOUNDS

SOFT "C"   =   "S" before E - I - Y

cEnt

cIty

cYcle

HARD "C"   =   "K" all other times:

cat, coat, cut, clock, cream, music

---

1. Give the 2 sounds of "C."

2. Know which "C" sound is SOFT & HARD.

3. Know which 3 letters control SOFT "C."

    NOTE EXCEPTION: The word, "facade"

187

SET 6. "G" HAS 2 SOUNDS

SOFT "C"   =   "S" before E - I - Y

SOFT "G"   =   "J" before E - I - Y

g E n t l e

g I r a f f e

g Y m

HARD "G"   =   "GUH" all other times:

gate, got, gun, glare, great, gag, vague

---

1. Give the 2 sounds of "G."

2. Know which "G" sound is SOFT & HARD.

3. Know which 3 letters control SOFT "G."

    NOTE EXCEPTIONS: The words "get, girl, hunger"

SET 7. 2 SOUNDS of "Q"

"Q"   =   "KW" as in QUEEN,
                    the MOST COMMON sound.

"Q"   is always followed by a "U"
                    and at least another vowel.

*4th Graders-up, know that

"QUE"   =   "K" as in CRITIQUE
                    on END of words

---

1. Know the 2 sounds of "Q."

2. Know that the letter "U" always follows "Q."

SET 8. 2 SOUNDS OF "X"

"KS" as in BOX   =   most COMMON sound

"Z" as in XEROX   =   BEGINNING of words

---

1. Say 2 sounds of "X."

SET 9. "Y" INFORMATION

"Y" can be BOTH a VOWEL & a CONSONANT

CONSONANT

"Y"   =   "YUH" as in YELLOW
at the BEGINNING of words.

VOWEL
("Y" is a VOWEL in the next 3.)

"Y"   =   "E" as in BABY
if on END of word, and NO VOWEL
IS RIGHT IN FRONT of the "Y."

"Y"   =   "I" as in MY
if "Y" is the ONLY vowel in the word.

"Y"   =   "Ø" as in DAY
NO SOUND when a VOWEL
is RIGHT IN FRONT OF "Y."

1. Memorize "crutch words" for ALL "Y" sounds.

2. Tell WHEN "Y" has its different sounds.

3. Know when "Y" is a CONSONANT & when it is a VOWEL.

SET 10. VOWEL COMBINATIONS

"OW-2"	=	COW, SN$\overline{\text{O}}$W
		(The COW is standing in the SN$\overline{\text{O}}$W.)
"OU"	=	OUT
*"EW"	=	FEW "$\overline{\text{U}}$"
		(A FEW people went to EUROPE.)
"EU"	=	EUROPE "$\overline{\text{U}}$"
"AW"	=	SAW (I SAW an AUTOmobile.)
"AU"	=	AUTO
"OI"	=	OIL
		(A BOY was putting OIL in the car.)
"OY"	=	BOY
"OO-2"	=	T$\overline{\text{OO}}$, L$\breve{\text{OO}}$K
		(She LOOKs like her mother, TOO.)
"UY"	=	BUY "$\overline{\text{I}}$" (Go BUY yourself a present.)
"EY-3"	=	"$\overline{\text{A}}$-$\overline{\text{E}}$-$\overline{\text{I}}$"
		(they-key-eye, or 1st 3 VOWELS)
"AIGH"	=	"$\overline{\text{A}}$" (str-AIGH-t)
"IGH"	=	"$\overline{\text{I}}$" (h-IGH)
"EIGH^2"	=	"$\overline{\text{A}}$-$\overline{\text{I}}$" (EIGH-t & h-EIGH-t)

---

1. Say sounds for ALL 14 Vowel Combinations, quickly and out of order.

2. Memorize "crutch words" and "silly" sentences.

3. Write (from memory) ALL Vowel Combinations.

4. *Sometimes, "ew" has the "oo" sound as in the word "blew."

NOTE: When A, E, O come right before W, W is a vowel.

4th Grade & Beyond Continue...

SET 11. FIRST VOWEL TALKS

Ā~~I~~ = TRAIN

Ā~~Y~~ = PLAY

Ē~~A~~ = TEACH

Ō~~A~~ = BOAT

Ō~~E~~ = TOE

* Ē~~I~~ = RECEIVE

---

1. Recognize the COMMON combinations of vowels when the FIRST VOWEL is LONG, and the SECOND is SILENT.

NOTE EXCEPTIONS: * "ei" in believe, rein, feign

SET 12. BOTH VOWELS TALK

IA = CALIFORNIA

IO = RADIO

IU = TRIUMPH

UI = TUITION

UA = INDIVIDUAL

EO = RODEO

EI = SPONTANEITY

---

1. Recognize these commonly called DIPTHONGS.

2. BOTH vowels talk in DIPTHONGS.

3. DIPTHONGS usually begin with "I" or "U."

SET 13. COMMON PREFIXES

mis ex un al semi ab

com tri es con dis sub

in tran ap sur re anti

a de ac be im pre ad

pro el co en ir inter

---

1. Pronounce PREFIXES quickly.

2. PREFIXES come at the BEGINNING of words.

3. Vowels on the END of PREFIXES are usually LONG.

SET 14. COMMON SUFFIXES

less	ment	ary	ance	ward	
iøus	tion	e	ēøus	able	
ety	er	ist	al	ing	ness
ed³	est	sion	tivø	ation	
ish	ion	øus	ity	tious	
xious	ful	tial	ant	cial	
cious	xion	cian	shion		

---

1. Pronounce SUFFIXES quickly.

2. Remember "E" on the end of SUFFIXES is SILENT.

3. "ed" has 3 sounds: wanted-ed, walked-t, cried-d.

4. "ion" says "yun" as in "onion."

5. tion, sion, shion, xion, cian   =   "shun."
   tious, cious, xious   =   "shus."
   tial, cial, shal   =   "shal."

SET 15. SILENT LETTERS

"K" before	"N"	=	KNOW
"G" before	"N"	=	GNAT
"P" before	"N"	=	PNEUMONIA
"P" before	"S"	=	PSYCHOLOGY
"W" before	"R"	=	WRITE
"T" before	"CH"	=	CATCH
"D" before	"GE"	=	HEDGE
"T" between	"SL"	=	WHISTLE
"B" after	"M"	=	THUMB
"H" after	"K"	=	KHAKI
"H" after	"R"	=	RHYME
"N" after	"M"	=	COLUMN

---

1. Be familiar with COMMON SILENT LETTERS.

2. Pronounce "crutch" words.

SET 16. SYLLABICATION RULES

V = VOWEL / C = CONSONANT

ba-by   1. VCV = V / CV

win-ter   2. VCCV = VC / CV

bicy-cle   3. C + LE = / CLE on END of word is the last syllable.

re-port   4. Separate PREFIXES & SUFFIXES from
resist-ant   the root word.

post-man 5. Divide between COMPOUND words.

   *   6. Never split words on RRA Cards #3, #4, & #10.

flow-er   7. Divide between 2 separate VOWEL SOUNDS.

---

1. Say the 7 SYLLABICATION RULES.

2. Be able to APPLY these rules in decoding.

3. * RRA Cards   #3   =   Vowels + R
                                #4   =   "H" Family
                         #10   =   Vowel Combinations

DRILL 1.

CONSONANT BLENDS & VOWELS

gro	bru	scra	bra	swo
ske	gli	twe	gra	
ste	pla	sli	gla	spe
tw	bre	swa	sco	fle
cre	clo	bla	sma	
tri	sca	tro	spu	dro
sna	dri	plo	gri	sto
fra	glu	cri	cla	whi

---

1. Pronounce at the rate of 1 PER SECOND, using a SHORT VOWEL at the end of the syllable.

2. Pronounce at the rate of 1 PER SECOND, using a LONG VOWEL at the end of the syllable.

DRILL 2.

CONSONANT BLENDS,
"H" FAMILY & SHORT VOWELS

chre	spra	thru	scro
sple	scri	squa	spro
shro	splu	scre	squi
thri	shre	phra	scru
spri	stro	shru	spli
stra	chro	thre	splo
chri	spre	squo	shra
stre	thra	sque	stri
phri	spl	thro	chra
whe	gha	whi	gho

1. Pronounce at the rate of 1 PER SECOND, using a SHORT VOWEL.

2. Pronounce at the rate of 1 PER SECOND, using a LONG VOWEL.

DRILL 3.

CONSONANTS + VOWELS + R, & VOWEL COMBINATIONS

gir	voy	tow	tar	loo
loi	bur	gaw	soo	mou
fur	sir	ber	mar	tey
cou	for	dir	har	soi
new	wow	roy	guy	fow
dew	dar	paw	boo	pur
hur	raw	wou	hew	pau

---

1. Pronounce at the rate of 1 PER SECOND.

DRILL 4.

CONSONANT BLENDS + VOWEL COMBINATIONS

smoo grau scou gloi

brew screy threw sprau

twou smeu plau speu

glau dreu staw clou

bleu grau schoo jigh

flaw snew flaigh skaw

stoy spou scraw pleu

gluy trau scoy freigh

---

1. Pronounce at the rate of 1 PER SECOND.

DRILL 5.

PHONIC QUIZ

ur	ar	or	er	ir	au	"c^2"
	oy	ew	ch^3	"y^4"	$eigh^2$	
	sh	ow^2	ey^3	"g^2"	igh	
		oo^2	ph	eu	"q^2"	
		ou	oi	"x^2"	gh^3	
	aigh	aw	th	wh	uy	

List the Silent Letters
When are Vowels long ?
When are "C" & "G" Soft ?
Give the 7 Syllabication Rules.
Give the short Vowel Sounds: a - e - i - o - u

1. Recite all phonic information at an age-appropriate speed.

Appendix C
Super Sleuth

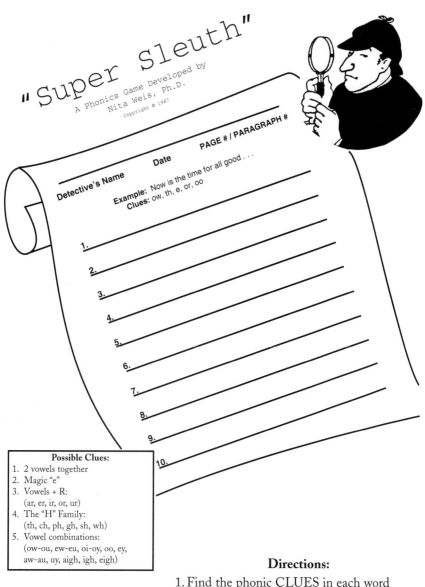

"Super Sleuth"

A Phonics Game Developed by
Nita Weis, Ph.D.
Copyright © 1987

Detective's Name _____   Date _____   **PAGE # / PARAGRAPH #** _____

Example: Now is the time for all good . . .
Clues: ow, th, e, or, oo

1. _____
2. _____
3. _____
4. _____
5. _____
6. _____
7. _____
8. _____
9. _____
10. _____

Possible Clues:
1. 2 vowels together
2. Magic "e"
3. Vowels + R:
   (ar, er, ir, or, ur)
4. The "H" Family:
   (th, ch, ph, gh, sh, wh)
5. Vowel combinations:
   (ow-ou, ew-eu, oi-oy, oo, ey,
   aw-au, uy, aigh, igh, eigh)

Directions:
1. Find the phonic CLUES in each word
2. List the CLUES for each word on the correct line.
3. Use a comma to separate between words.
4. See possible clues in box to left
5. **Super Sleuth** Badge to winner

207

Appendix D
Word Busters

WORD BUSTERS

A SYLLABICATION GAME
Developed by Nita Weis, Ph.D.
Copyright © 1987

WORDS	SYLLABLES	POINTS
1.		
2.		
3.		
4.		
5.		
Total Points		

RULES

SYLLABICATION RULES
(V = vowel, C = consonant)

ba-by	1. VCV = V - CV
win-ter	2. VCCV = VC- CV
bi-cy-cle	3. C + LE = -CLE
re-sist-ant	4. SPLIT OFF PREFIXES & SUFFIXES
post-man	5. DIVIDE COMPOUND WORDS
	* 6. NEVER SPLIT RRA CARDS #3, 4, 10
flow-er	7. SPLIT 2 SEPARATE VOWEL SOUNDS
	* Vowels + "R"
	"H" Family
	Vowel Combinations

SCORING

Students earn ONE point for EACH SYLLABLE for EACH word that he/she CORRECTLY . . .

    divides,
    gives rules, and
    pronounces.

Student with the highest score wins!

NAME   TEAM   DATE

211

Appendix E
Mind Maps

NOTE
These mind maps were originally hand drawn, but for visual
clarity, they were redrawn by computer.
Your child will use these for ideas and examples
to create his own.

213

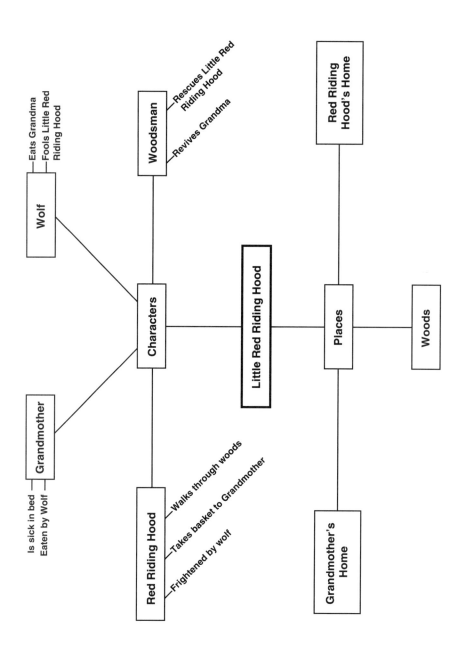

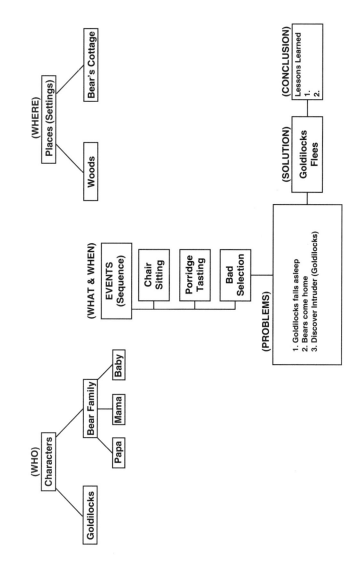

PRIMARY LEVEL BOOK REPORT MAP

(WHO)
Characters

Goldilocks

Bear Family

Papa | Mama | Baby

(WHERE)
Places (Settings)

Woods | Bear's Cottage

(WHAT & WHEN)
EVENTS (Sequence)

Chair Sitting

Porridge Tasting

Bad Selection

(PROBLEMS)

1. Goldilocks falls asleep
2. Bears come home
3. Discover Intruder (Goldilocks)

(SOLUTION)
Goldilocks Flees

(CONCLUSION)
Lessons Learned
1.
2.

GOLDILOCKS & The THREE BEARS

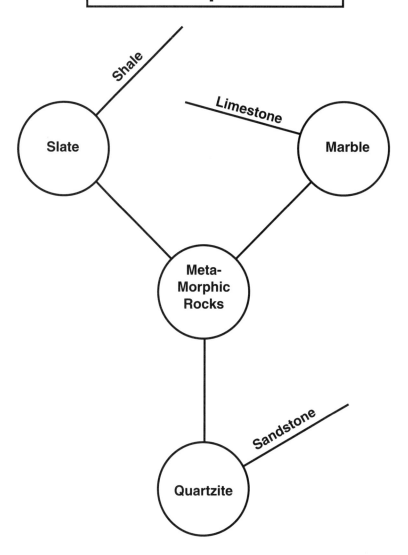

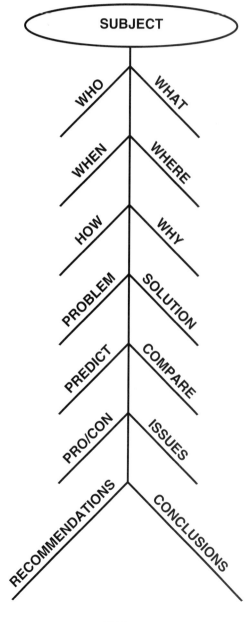

Memory Minder

SUBJECT

WHO
WHAT
WHEN
WHERE
HOW
WHY
PROBLEM
SOLUTION
PREDICT
COMPARE
PRO/CON
ISSUES
RECOMMENDATIONS
CONCLUSIONS

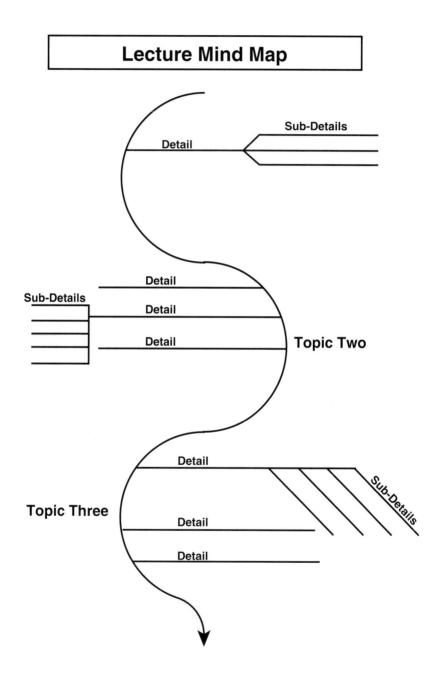

Lecture Mind Map

Detail

Sub-Details

Detail

Detail

Detail

Sub-Details

Topic Two

Detail

Sub-Details

Topic Three

Detail

Detail

1. Early Warning Clouds

2. Immediate Bad Weather Clouds

3. Weather Predicting Clouds

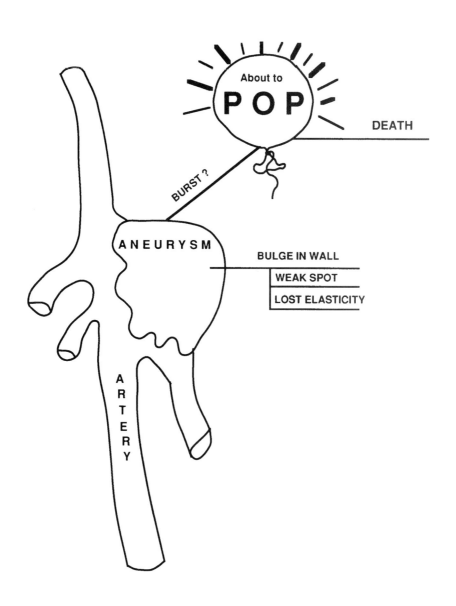

Religion

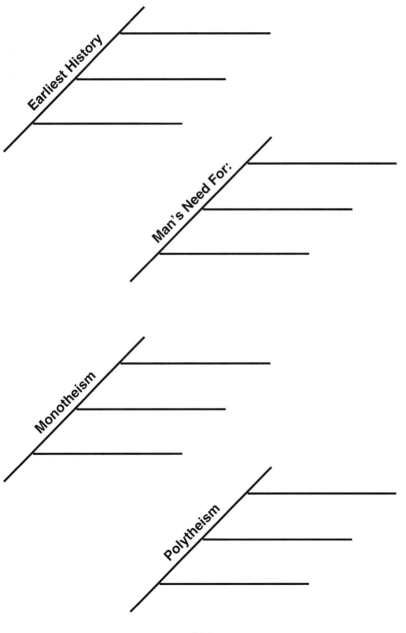

Earliest History

Man's Need For:

Monotheism

Polytheism

Development of Public Schools

Need Better Schools

Cities

Finance

Taxes

Church

John Dewey

Universities

Problems

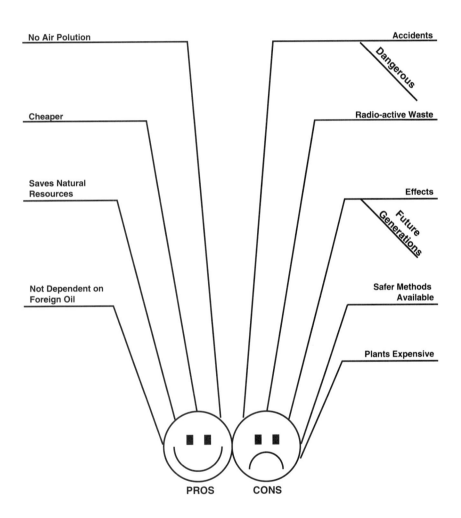

Appendix F
Responsibility Contract

RESPONSIBILITY CONTRACT

Developed by Dr. Nita Weis, Ph.D. © 1987

PARENTS' NOTES:

A. Determine the acceptable Achievement/Behavioral levels, in accordance with your child's test findings and in consultation with an educational professional.

B. Exercise restraint in helping the child with homework. "Occasional" clarification/explanation/math drill-card quizzing/dictation of spelling words is permissible, so long as "emotions" are kept at an acceptable level.

C. Provide for a study station, well equipped with all the necessary, age-appropriate (and affordable) "study stuff" and organizational materials, such as: computer, calculator, desk or table, white marker board, colored dry-erase markers, high lighters, 3" x 5" index cards, lots of pencils, sharpeners, notebook paper, notebook dividers, stapler, paper clips, manila folders, etc.

D. Approve a daily homestudy session time, one-to-two hours a day, depending on the age-grade of your child. This schedule need not be the same time each day, but must be followed, once set. Study sessions, if at all possible, should be completed prior to the evening meal.

E. Parents, do not assume the role of homework detective: "Have you done your homework?" Instead, the child is the reporter: "Mom, Dad, here is my completed homework. May I be excused from my study session?"

F. Never take forgotten homework to school for your child.

G. Expect to experience *Helicopter-Mother Withdrawal,* Moms or Dads who, innocently, *hover* too closely over their children.

H. Recognize and reward academic and behavioral improvement. BUT be aware that *inflated* praise compromises the development of independent study habits and responsibility.

I. Objectives must be clearly stated and posted.

J. Objectives must include two basic components:
   1. Something to start doing; and
   2. Something to stop doing. Focus on about three objectives.

K. Assign a timeline for all objectives. Example: Child will do whatever, by designated time, proved by
   _____.

L. Act on the knowledge that all behavior is maintained by its consequences. Therefore, child is to be informed in advance of specific consequences for objectives not met.

M. Allowances should be "on hold" until such time as objectives are being met on a regular basis.

Starting the Contract

1. Child takes contract (in an unsealed envelope) to school on Mondays and gives contract to teacher(s).

2. Child picks up contract on Fridays from teacher(s) and brings contract home to parents.

3. If contract objectives were met for the entire week, as indicated by teacher initials and signature, child exchanges contract for meal ticket for the regular family menu for the following week.

4. However, if contract objectives were not met for the week, or if child forgot to pick up the contract from the teacher, the child has selected the vegetable menu for the evening meal, *for the next 7 days.* This procedure is followed until such time as the child is able to meet classroom objectives five days in a row!

5. The vegetable menu may consist of any assortment of vegetables that the child hates! Only one vegetable per evening meal. Vegetables may be served raw or cooked, with salt only added. No sauces or dressings may be added to make them more tasty. Suggested vegetables: boiled okra, raw broccoli, cauliflower, turnip greens, spinach, squash, asparagus, cabbage, whatever your child already hates!

6. Water is the only beverage allowed at the evening meal.

7. Child may eat the vegetable menu along with the family at the evening meal. However, no complaints are allowed regarding the vegetable menu, since it was the child's decision to break the contract. Should child tend to gag on the vegetables, he is allowed to leave the table. Absolutely nothing to eat or drink is given until breakfast, except water.

8. No food or beverage, other than water, is to be eaten by child after lunch. Take whatever precautions are necessary to see that this is followed, i.e.:

   a. Person picking up child from school must be aware of the *dietary* guidelines.

      b. Child cannot be given money that could be spent for food.

      c. Family, friends, siblings must not furnish the child *care packages.*

9. Child is told frequently, pleasantly, and calmly that the vegetable therapy is being used as a reminder of the wrong decisions he made in failing to meet his contract objectives.

10. SUGGESTION: Moms, serve the child's favorite foods over the next two weeks. Aromas of his favorite foods should permeate the home. The regular and vegetable menus should be posted side-by-side. The object is to "tantalize the child's olfactory nerves."

11. The Positive s ide of Vegetable Therapy:

      a. Behavior turnaround is quick, usually within two weeks, if parents are consistent in following the guidelines.

      b. Parents are relieved of responsibilities that should be the child's.

      c. Vegetable Therapy does not make kids hate vegetables since the only vegetables used are those he already hates!

We solemnly affirm that we've read carefully all of the parent notes regarding the responsibility contract. We agree to follow these guidelines, consistently, even when we experience the normal, frequent, loving, parental urges to gather up our child in our arms and stuff him with delicious goodies!

_____

Mother's Signature   Date

_____

Father's Signature   Date

STUDENT AGREEMENT

PARENTS:
READ THESE STATEMENTS TO YOUR CHILD, PARAPHRASING INTO AGE-APPROPRIATE WORDS.

I understand and agree that the goals of this contract will help me to accept responsibility for my decisions at home and school that affect my learning.

I understand that I eat the same foods as the family for evening meals IF I meet my week-to-week contract objectives.

I also understand that if I fail to meet these goals on a week-to-week basis, the only food or beverage after lunch will be vegetables and water, for 7 days in a row.

I also agree that it is my responsibility to do my own homework, at my study station, without help from my parents. If I do not understand how to do my homework, it is my responsibility to ask my teacher or a classmate, prior to leaving school on the day of the assignment.

It is also my responsibility to bring all materials and assignments home regarding my homework, and to take my completed assignments back to school, on time. If I forget, I am responsible for the consequences.

_____

Child's Name   Date

NOTE TO PARENTS: Xerox a number of copies of the following contract and keep the original for future use.

TEACHERS: Please do not discuss the contract with the student or let him see you marking the contract. The student is fully aware of the contract guidelines. But, if he finds out that he's "blown it" early in the week, he may figure he may as well "goof off" the rest of the week, because he's getting an "alternative menu" for dinner for the next 7 days.

On Friday, please place the contract in a sealed envelope before giving it to the student. Behavior turnaround usually takes about two weeks!

RESPONSIBILITY CONTRACT

OBJECTIVES	M	T	W	TH	F
Teachers, please initial each day if objectives were met.					
1. Demonstrates a positive attitude towards learning	___	___	___	___	___
2. Demonstrates self-control	___	___	___	___	___
3. Demonstrates responsibility for assignments	___	___	___	___	___
4. Works at ability level	___	___	___	___	___

If work is below expectancy for child's ability, please circle area of concern: tests, class work, homework, other.

_____

_____

_____

_____

_____

_____

Teachers Comments

_____

Teacher's Signature   Date